Werkstatt Neue Kultur/New Culture Workshop
Telotopia

Abridged version in smart print

AF211151

Werkstatt Neue Kultur
New Culture Workshop

Project and educational workshop for a new culture

Permanent staff:
Andreas Poggel: Mediation & Nonviolent communication
Christoph W. Rosenthal: Projects – Research – Art

www.werkstatt-neue-kultur.net

The "New Culture Workshop" has so far been active only in a small circle in Germany. Our home pages and texts are so far therefore available in German only. However, you may contact us in English or in Dutch. We'll see what possibilities the future will hold in store for us.

English Translation by **Peter Geiger**
Translation service available from: newculture@freenet.de

Werkstatt Neue Kultur
New Culture Workshop

Christoph W. Rosenthal & Andreas Poggel (eds.)
English Translation by Peter Geiger

Telotopia

A cultural-architectural sketch of a desirable culture of the future

- Outline of Telotopistics

Abridged version
in smart print

Bibliographical information of the German National Library:
The German National Library lists this publication in the German
National Biography; detailed bibliographical data can be obtained via
the Internet at http://dnb.dnb.de. =

Bibliografische Information der Deutschen Nationalbibliothek:
Die Deutsche Nationalbibliothek verzeichnet diese Publikation in der
Deutschen Nationalbibliografie; detaillierte bibliografische Daten sind
im Internet über http://dnb.dnb.de abrufbar.

Publisher/Verlag: BoD · Books on Demand GmbH,
In de Tarpen 42, 22848 Norderstedt

Printed by/ Druck: Libri Plureos GmbH, Friedensallee 273,
22763 Hamburg

Made und printed in Germany
ISBN: 978-3-7693-0618-7

Outline

A desirable culture of the future.

The magnificent advantage that we have today in spite of all difficulties is that we don't have to accept any longer historically created conditions and notions like the world as a disk. The overview of history and human evolution far exceeding primates has by now enabled us to understand the emergent errors and wrong courses taken; and, both in human-social and technological-economic terms, we now have enough potential available for a desirable culture of the future.

Some people have already made a start in this direction, personally and in smaller circles. We, too, have been experimenting personally for a longer time and can now build on some experience and insights. Utilizing existing space and opportunities for developments of a desirable culture of the future is a good idea.

However, to ensure that this does not merely amount to cultivating personal privileges, which is ultimately one of the reasons of the historical problem, it's important to develop a conception of what would actually constitute a desirable culture in the overall social portfolio.

Beyond the personal, a cultural-architectural debate is definitely needed as to which direction societal development should actually take. The mere conception of life becoming "fabulous" is not even sufficient for building a single family home common in our world. Such mindless "practice" was no longer sufficient in human evolutionary development. In this, humans differed from animals.

Human evolutionary development became feasible only through a cultural concept generally considered to be desirable and an essential reason for historical problems is that this "practice" took on a life of its own.

But in view of the complexity of the human brain only a culture based on collaborative communication will create social stability at a desirable level over tens of thousands of years. Precisely in this development lay the secret of success of human evolutionary development with its result in our species, Homo sapiens. Everything else "following chimpanzees" succumbed to failure.

A desirable culture of the future needs a cultural-architectural blueprint in which the static requirements of human disposition towards behavior and needs have been processed in the overall structure of a communicable form. Not all details need – and even *may* – not be resolved. Objective as well as social resolution of the cultural-architectural basic feature and constitution are crucial.

Telotopia is designed to be an introduction to developing a corresponding cultural architecture of concepts and practice. Some potential of desirable features is already available, as can perhaps be illustrated through the added photos here.

The social and human confusion that emerged is not necessary. Building a New Culture is possible!

Table of Contents

3 On the Biographical Structure of Telotopia

4 The Entire Telotopia Complex

Preface

With Telotopia, "New Culture Workshop" intends to illustrate, based on a cultural-architectural example, what a desirable culture of the future might mean to us in the overall social outcome.

Now we are happy to be able to also provide an English edition in order to contribute a corresponding debate to other countries; where possible, even to other cultures of ancient traditions. For these traditions may contribute a different potential which is also of paramount significance to the evolution of Telotopia. If favorable opportunities should arise for us, we would also like to publish editions in more languages.

"Telotopia" and "New Culture" are about a human history perspective. "Culture" was the novel human dimension of human evolutionary development of personality, social and relationship life including all creativity and quality of life. It emerged through detachment from genetic behavior control by virtue of language, communication, and acquisition of the ability of self-control.

"New Culture" is about processing historical evolution both of progress and the various consequences of loss of culture, as is demonstrated with sexism, racism, violence, power, social hierarchies, exploitation, and barbarism through to slavery, dictatorship, fascism, and war. All these problems are definitely not a relict of evolution or human nature – quite the contrary, they are the inevitable consequence of an insufficient or incapable installation of the human software named "culture", particularly with the operating system level of behavior control, spiritual development, and communication.

Basically, the problem of loss of culture emerged during the gigantic natural disasters at the end of the Ice Age that lasted over three millennia. This has resulted in many consequential effects – actually, until today. But there is now enough food, products, service offers, and production options. As already established during the 1830s, the economic problem results from a surplus. What is really lacking is what is actually meant by "culture", viewed from the cultural disposition of our species, Homo sapiens: a capable relationship and social life, as well as sufficient personal acquisition of the ability to communicate, as in genuine and humanly sufficient communication.

The "New Culture Workshop" would like to provide contributions towards the development of a new culture. "Telotopia" is about a cultural-architectural design of how a desirable culture of the future might look like. The question in this context is not primarily how this design might be realized in view of the political-economic realities. Initially, it must be about resolutions of what is realistically understood as "desirable" beyond the various individual moments. What is initially needed is a generally resolved blueprint of a New Culture.

This model may be of effective relevance to the various projects. It can show in a new manner that various projects are of significance for developing a "desirable culture of the future", and also which. It may contribute to connecting various approaches, even if in concrete life people are pursuing completely different paths. Like an architectural blueprint of a huge project, a more sophisticated cultural architecture may demonstrate where the various locations and paths converge one day. From there the concern of numerous projects and individuals becomes much more comprehensible.

With this in mind, the "New Culture Workshop" wants to further promote and develop this examination through exchange, networks, presentations, events, etc. More project conceptions are available here.

This work is meant to be only a beginning. Sadly, for the moment we cannot offer a better format of this book as yet. We probably have far more and better image material, but not the copyrights to enable us to use it.

This abridged version is meant to provide an initial impression of the new approach to cultural architecture. Above all, the in-depth justifications and explanations of this design have been abridged here. In this manner, the visual character of this cultural-architectural design comes out even more prominently and, moreover, the abridged version is cheaper. Moreover, initially, this edition has been produced using a cheap printing procedure to enable us to send some copies for free to interesting addresses (the better print version would cost €4 - 5 per copy). Further, we will create an even more abridged and most of all data reduced version for sending via e-mail.

For further debates of the social notions of the future and goals, the in-depth justifications and explanations are without doubt essential. But at the moment, starting off with such debates is important. On the corresponding resonance, augmenting publications are conceivable and also intended.

In charge of writing and design: C. Rosenthal.

For **New Culture Workshop**

Christoph W. Rosenthal and Andreas Poggel

Preface for the people of cultures of ancient traditions

The writing and the photos of this book are certainly connected to conditions in Germany. However, the idea of Telotopia should especially also be of significance to cultures of ancient traditions.

The basic ideas of Telotopia have also been inspired by examples of ancient cultures, and this context also has its method in that the debate of a desirable culture of the future builds on insights of the human evolutionary disposition of Man and the corresponding culture of the Ice Age.

This view certainly does not reject progress. However, it is to be established that many historical developments were in fact results from natural disasters and emergencies, as well as power, wars, and violence, which will have to be dismantled for a desirable culture of the future.

The general principle of Telotopia is to establish conditions that enable again social organization in real social self-determination and in communal communication and that are also mostly capable of self-sufficiency. According to scientific insights, this would most of all need social conditions that are humanly manageable, as they existed in tribes and locations in former times. With his "village republics", Mohandas Gandhi, too, took a similar view that is still to play a role in India. Specifically, this is a question of the respective natural conditions. Our system of independent social associations, here referred to as "Boro", comprises an average overall size of about 4,000 people consisting of independent sub-units.

But this "Boro" is the central political entity in the shape of a present "state" within which social self-organization is possible, but which on the other hand also provides the decision-making basis for democratic determination of the organization of global conditions, such as in distributing land, resources, and production goods.

The Boro enables self-determination of one's own conditions without being isolated because of it. According to the concept of Telotopia, each Boro is, in global conditions, equally entitled to have a say, to have an equal share in the resources of the world and to land with enough resources for self-organization. But in reverse, a Boro does not have the sovereignty of present-day states: no Boro has the right to ruin the environment, to violate human rights, and to attack the territories of other Boros. Should, due to climate change, for example, a loss of one's territory or problems regarding sufficient supplies occur, these problems must be resolved, depending on their extent, at a respectively working higher administrative level of the Boro organization, if necessary, via the world Boro council.

Perhaps it becomes clear already at this point which significance this concept might have especially for cultures of ancient tradition.

Telotopia may point a way to the future here where cultures of ancient tradition will not only hopelessly lag behind the centers of the global market and be and remain dependent on charity help to survive. Rather, the ancient cultures will be given a completely new meaning here.

For the concept of Telotopia, the cultures of ancient tradition will provide huge experience for a desirable culture of the future. From this perspective, the people of the cultures of ancient tradition are interesting dialogue partners to us. They may, in practical terms, even be the special pioneers on the way to Telotopia. Many parts of the world have, in various aspects, much more potential for developments in the context of Telotopia than our industrial societies and cityscapes that are in part highly built-up.

We of the New Culture Workshop appreciate cultures of ancient tradition and hope for mutually enhancing dialogues.

Personal Remarks

As the initiator and moderator of the discussion regarding Telotopia at the "New Culture Workshop" as well as author or final editor of this book, I would like to precede it with some information on how this project emerged. For this has a longer history now.

My explicit discussion of the topic of Utopia started off in the context when, at the end of March 1980, we established an apartment-sharing situation as a group of 8 people in Göttingen, Germany. This enabled me to gain speedy access to the most varied of alternative projects such as to a publisher, to newspapers, and a host of contacts. Even if a lot of it had not yet fully matured back then, this opened up perspectives to me which I found worth pursuing. Since I saw realistic opportunities for this, my decision in summer 1981 was in favor of a correspondingly free way of living.

However, this trend back then did not last for too long in this shape and so, after my course at university, I found myself confronted with a variety of requirements, not least regarding the question of the economic prospect. Even if discussion of utopia continued to be of significance both in terms of content as well as in practical terms, it was not until the end of the 1990s that I got around to dealing with how my utopia might look in societal terms. Until then, the book *Ecotopia* had, among others, been an inspiration to me. While working at my own design, however, I found that the discussion of "utopia" now contained two different dimensions. In both regards, I no longer considered the book *Ecotopia* satisfactory.

One dimension was connected to my personal life history. This related most of all to the areas of education, art/cultural items, and shared housing or communal living. However, since I had already taken up this path of life as early as 1980, after nearly 20 years (and from today's perspective, after more than 40 years), this dimension of utopia took a quite different turn than at the beginning. This was no longer the remote view that could be infinitely adorned with imaginations, but it had long become transparent how much everything depended on the respective people and realities. And here, despite all planning, one will quickly meet one's limitations (e.g., time and money), as they are more generally known here. My experience probably flows into the present concept. But this dimension is not the question here.

Thus, I became attentive to the other dimension of the topic. During my script work, I noticed that that which was of interest to me regarding "utopia" was the draft of a truly possible model of a desirable culture of the future: the evolution of a cultural architecture that deals, analogous to the architecture of buildings, with the overall social system.

The first draft in this form emerged in spring 1998. Although it already contained the core elements of the present draft, it was much more in its infancy back then. In contrast to this, I reached a different level with my second draft of winter 2009/2010. It was already called Telotopia, and contained the essential features of the current version. But prior to publishing my work on human evolution and on history, which provide a certain basis for this, I wanted to qualify further first, which was to delay it even further than expected.

Taking the results of my research, my view is that the evolution of a desirable culture with a permanent social stability in peace, social and personal self-determination and full quality of living is still a genuine human possibility, nay, in a certain respect, it is only possible today: a permanent future perspective for the first time. My hope is therefore for some lively exchange regarding our visions, ideas, and experience.

Christoph Rosenthal

1   Introduction:

On the basics of Telotopia
(significantly abridged in this version)

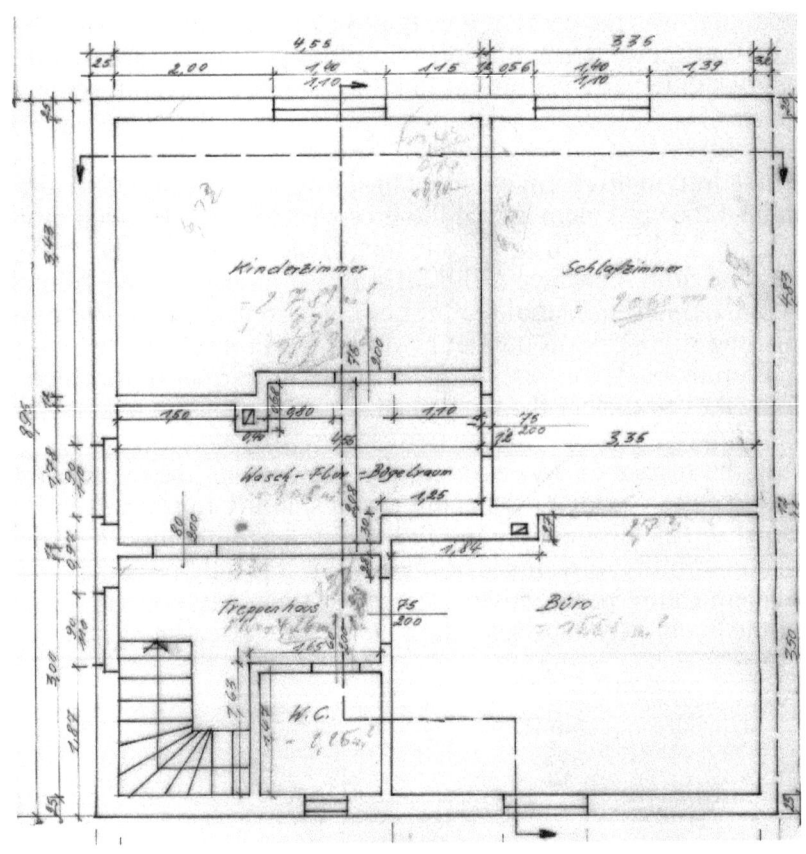

Architectural plan (detail)

1.1 Culture, utopia, and telopistics

Due to Man's cultural disposition, the topic of Utopia has been of fundamental importance from time immemorial; as part of mythologies, it has always been a key and crucial social element of culture. Historically, of course, it was monopolized and distorted right from the start by the new political ideology and later economic advertising. In a certain way, the current extent of utopian images in economic and political propaganda has become a fundamental problem where unsatisfied needs are exploited in themselves in order to deceive about the actual problems.

However, initially, we have to find that already human evolutionary development at its last stage towards our species, Homo sapiens, is explained exclusively through a preceding Utopia of humanly oriented and capable social conditions. Else, people would not have been able to go beyond the social problems of genetically inherited behavior forms which doomed the evolutionarily preceding hominids to extinction in spite of their great technological intelligence and its broad promulgation across the globe. It also required a motivating objective of a productive relationship and social life that met with enough appreciation. It was only with a "Utopia" that offered enough understanding for a desirable life and behavior that the human evolutionary process enabled people to overcome the inherited social conditions and behavior forms that evolutionarily ended with extinction.

This Utopia emerged from the original mythology. It was the stories told to *infants* from which social Utopia emerged. Just as these stories, quite as infants wanted to hear them, told of the "primeval mother moon" who specially created this world for them for the purpose of happiness and love, so these stories even offered adults themselves the idea of something better being possible than making life difficult for each other, like the hominids, through constant competitive fights, and eventually ruining it.

Unlike the other biological processes of evolution, human evolution cannot be explained in terms of natural processes. What mattered in human evolution was *detachment* from the biological mechanisms of genetic behavioral control. The evolutionary acquisition of the capability of self-control was solely possible due to a communally determined culture and objective. The initial cue was offered by mythological stories that infants wanted to hear due to their ongoing linguistic development. Their motifs of care, solidarity, and a "good life" provided the basics of the original Utopia.

Thus, Man always has a *pre*-requisite for this course of development. But as a consequence of human evolutionary development of Man's culturality, this pre- is also always "utopian" and goal-oriented (Greek telos = goal>> teleology, telotopy). This is where the great significance of Ernst Bloch's contributions come in, e.g. "The Principle of Hope". *Man* can never be understood solely in terms of biology and the past. It is always orientations, hopes, and goals that are also connected to human self-control, similar to driving a car. Where there are no hopes and no real objectives, there is no actual self-control but only reacting.

Without a communally clarified construction plan of a social life there would never, in human evolutionary terms, have arisen a capable social life = culture (in its actual, biological sense) and therefore our cultural species of Homo sapiens. This is all the more true today with regards to social life.

Here, one can view the relationship of Utopia and telotopistics very much as a type of an architectural project. This project starts with Utopia; Utopia triggers the project. It appears as the initial expression of an actual project with more complex objectives. In social contexts, it is a good and important thing to initially tap these purely subjective dimensions of one's wishes, needs, and imaginations without immediately thinking about feasibility, which should not get out of sight, of course. The better one understands one's wishes and needs with regard to the objectives, the closer one can approach them via the results, even if not everything can be (immediately) actualized.

18

In the same manner, architecture initially plays with imaginations. If a specific leitmotif or model has become clear in the process, the second step will be taken in architecture to work out these ideas to turn them into a real construction plan. In this very manner, telotopistics can be understood as cultural architecture. The difference is merely that it refers to *one* or, as in this case, *the* social *complex on a world scale*.

With the social complex, however, we still have to deal with a dimension of its own today. The question of how a cultural-architectural overall model of a desirable culture of the future might be **actualized** in *politico-economic terms* must be seen as an entire controversy of its own. In any event, it is explicitly ***not*** a part of this book.

The prerequisite for the vision of Telotopia building a human-democratic culture is to initially develop – precisely as with building a house – a *real model* of these objectives in order to enable the corresponding discussions about these objectives. The mere intention of life becoming "fabulous" is not even sufficient for building a single family home common in our world.

1.2 The Utopia may not be determined in advance

Here we can only give our unqualified consent to the view that the Utopia cannot and may not be determined in advance. Because all people of all generations have the right to determine their own lives in joint agreement.

Given our disposition as Homo sapiens, this is even an inevitable necessity if one does not want to lose control of one's circumstances. Ever since his human evolutionary detachment from the genetic behavioral control, Man has been predisposed towards a capable self-control in collaborative communication. Where this is not achieved but even turned off in an authoritarian manner (using the corresponding ideologies of all types), even more devastating consequences than high drunkenness on the wheel will soon become social reality, as has been dramatically demonstrated by the Third Reich in every aspect.

However, the problem was indeed that most Utopian designs of the past were oriented towards authoritarian control or actualization, just as revolutions were quickly turning into dictatorships.

This objection to such Utopian designs is probably absolutely correct so far. Now it's also important to consider that our conditions are built on an authoritarian foundation of customs, laws, property, etc. originating at the end of the Ice Age (about 12,000 to 10,000 years ago in the Near East) which has to this day dictated our realities in social life.

Although the new social organization, based on authoritarian-mytho-logical premisses (initially named "tribe"), initially offered secure supplies and social life among the chaotic circumstantial problems of the gigantic natural cataclysms at the end of the Ice Age, what was initially a "service to the people" was, in the course of historical development, turning into authoritarian structures for "progressive" cultures (initially in the Near East), with power and violence (right up to slavery) (see the Ancient Orient). In many respects, these principles were enshrined in the customs, laws, and social regulations that to this day stand in the way of actual democratic determination of our social conditions.

The cultural-architectural designs of telotopistics are not, as before, about decisions that interfere with the self-determination of future generations – as this is already the case with excessive use of resources and accumulation of waste and toxic fabrics.

Rather, it is about the discussion about what conditions are necessary for guaranteeing the right to self-determination of *all* people as permanently as possible, albeit taking reality into consideration. In other words, it is about designs that may enable a genuine, full and permanent actualization of human rights, of democracy and also ecological basics. For after the insights into human evolutionary development, only conditions that match human nature (> anthropology) and are controlled on the basis of collaborative communication can evade social ruin in the long run. Given the downright complex neurological disposition of Man, dictatorial forms are simply not suited for this (beyond a short order in emergencies).

Foregoing a cultural-architectural discussion and planning shows even graver consequences than foregoing a construction plan on building a common detached house, which is quite simple as opposed to the former. The mountains of debts of public households are also inevitable when starting to build a modern house without a real idea.

This is not about "back to nature" but rather "back to culture". Because the end of the Ice Age saw substantial losses of culture, with consequences lasting to this day, wherein the problems of power and violence are rooted with our species, Homo sapiens.

It takes a cultural architecture to resolve these problems socially and ecologically. This must be developed on the one hand from the positive insights into the human disposition (anthropology including psychology, neurology, etc.) and on the other hand, negatively (in what to avoid) from the appreciation of the causes of and backgrounds to the historical problems. To my mind, there are enough cues that can be made fruitful for a desirable culture of the future. The rest is up to our communication.

1.3   On the concept of Telotopia

Overall the concept of Telotopia is based on insights from human evolution, human sciences, history, and experience of the most varied of cultures.

In any event, this concept is not simply and not immediately built on our present civilizational culture, because this will not attain a solution of the existing problems. But Telotopia is not designed to be a "back to the Stone Age" prior to historical development.

Some not inconsiderable changes will come up with us anyway, probably as early as during the next couple of years. Such changes are, of course, never "easy". But without some changes the solutions to existing problems cannot be achieved, because we are living way beyond our means, in ecological, social and economic terms, which cannot go well for much longer.

From the insights into the causes of the historical problems, the requirements for the cultural reconstruction are by no means slight. This will definitely affect some habits and areas of luxury. But in many respects, the previous way of living can be definitely continued from the point of view of individuals. At the individual level, a completely different and unfamiliar culture will be introduced here.

Above all, Telotopia does not mean a mere waiving and loss; nor does it mean retrogression. On the contrary, it is about genuine progress as optimization of *actual* quality of life. Life in Telotopia probably tends to be simpler on the exterior, though not poorer but less complicated: less boogaboo and competitive fighting, and more freedom, cultural potential, relationship living, and satisfying actual needs.

In principle, all original and socially productive ways of life are possible in Telotopia: the *hunter-gatherer* culture, nomadic life, *horticulture*, rural, domestic, artisan life; living within nature and *urban* living including high-tech and industrial production.

The restrictions emerging in Telotopia will only result from the reality principle of natural principles of permanently oriented approaches and from the fact that self-determination of one's life should be open to everyone and not just to a few privileged at the cost of the rest of humanity. At any rate, that's the crucial key to these discussions and the concept presented here.

Of course, this is not to say that everything will be possible, and immediately so. But the culture of Telotopia is, from its insights into human nature, oriented in such a manner that people support each other in fulfilling their needs, because only in this manner will the optimum of quality of life and a permanent living social stability be achieved.

From these insights into the historical problem that led to fascism, wars, and cultural breakdowns arise two corresponding poles with regard to the solution which also play a key part for Telotopia.

The one pole is linked to the social basis. Under extended natural conditions, the old form of the "tribe" can, with collaborative communication, be considered and taken as such a basis. With a higher population number, as is the case with our world, a different concept is inevitable, however.

This novel concept is called "Boro" here. This is a historically novel mixture of village, urbanity, and – with regard to *its own self-organization* – an independent city state with about 4,000 inhabitants. Larger cities are formed as the type of a "county district" or, in our present world, "boroughs" from an association of some Boros (see below), but the decision-making authority rests with the Boros.

The other pole is linked to a global networking of Boros. In Telotopia, this Boro concept has been designed with other organizational structures *from below* via multiple levels up to the global level. It is only where the global level has been reached in such a structure that the problem of dictatorships, wars and violent battles for resources or even for "power" can be considered overcome. How such a global organizational structure built upon the Boros might look will be discussed in Part 4.

It is only when connecting both poles that the solution of the historical problem can be perceived. It is only an effective foundation in manageable independent social structures that ensures a general democracy, culture, and the possibility of a genuine personal self-determination.

The Boros are dependent on a larger networking organization. But this need not necessarily end up getting out of control of this super-organization and the pathological problem of "power". As long as the foundation of a general collaborative communication is correct, everything else desirable can be built on it.

1.4 Basic Law of the Telotopian constitution

Preamble

The complex of Telotopia is meant to be, mentally as well as materially, the actualization of human rights. It is beholden to a human social life, protection of individual personalities, as well as conservation of nature. It strives to enable humane life in freedom and mutual nurturance, i.e., from the point of view of our present conditions, that which must be understood as "culture" from human evolutionary development.

Paragraph 1 Basic Law

(1) The principle of human rights is rooted in providing conditions suitable for children through to enabling complete self-control in adolescence.

(2) The regulation of conditions suitable for children is made (a) according to the insights of the humanities (anthropology, psychology, etc.) and (b) according to the concrete needs of children, as enunciated by them (consent, etc.).

(3) The principle of conditions suitable for children also refers to the corresponding cultural offers made to children.

Paragraph 2 Basic Law

(1) Every human shall be, by dint of their person, fully entitled to share in the existing resources: sufficient nutrition, sufficient living space, meaningful and self-determined activities, and sufficient care in case of sickness and nursing care.

(2) Every human shall be, upon reaching maturity, fully entitled to self-determination within the framework of the Telotopian constitution (human rights + nature conservation).

(3) The pursuit of personal self-actualization within the framework of the Telotopian constitution shall be supported and promoted where possible.

(4) Any type of constraint that does not arise from reality itself shall be precluded. Exceptions shall only be admissible with neurological diseases (insanity, etc.), the prevention of offenses, and with problems due to natural disasters.

(5) Self-determination shall be accompanied by full entitlement to private property inasmuch as this refers to the sphere of the purely personal.

(6) Private property of land and public institutions shall be precluded. Economic independence can only refer to individuals themselves. This principle shall also be valid with regard to inheritance law.

Paragraph 3 Basic Law

(1) Social life of Telotopia shall be oriented towards ecological permanence.

(2) In the event of an acute conflict, the principle of Telotopian human rights shall override the realities of nature. *

(3) Human interference with nature shall be low.

(4) Further increase in population shall, with possible exceptions in uncharted territories, be precluded. Accordingly, the right of woman shall be generally limited to two children (see Dictionary part: → 5.1).

Paragraph 4 Basic Law

(1) The basic form of social organization is linked to the Boro within the framework of a global networking organization.

(2) Political sovereignty shall rest, as part of the Telotopian constitution, with the Boros. As part of this constitution, each Boro shall be entitled to self-determination of its social conditions. The Boros determine the superordinate organization in a format built from below (see Part 4).

(3) The Boro shall be created at a size that is socially manageable and that allows self-organization in collaborative communication.

(4) The superordinate organization right through to global networking organization is carried out in the mandate of the Boros and via the representative chosen by the Boros.

---

*Note: Population size and density, with living space and food production, already constitute interference with nature; however, this is unavoidable so far.

(5) Construction of the superordinate organization of the Boros shall be, from below upwards, in authorities according to the geographic contexts (districts, counties, states (cantons, provinces), countries, etc.).

Here's an extract from the **constitution** of the Ngarinyin Aboriginals that probably dates to the Paleolothic:

"Nobody living outside the sharing system
Kids ... wives ... husbands
All inside... everything all inside
Birds... every animal... dog
every living creature
it is all in the Wunan [...]
always be in the Wunan, doesn't matter what language [...]
they share it out... in the Wunan
Wunan sharing system for everything
Give right channel... nobody outside the channel
all... everybody family in one Wunan
Yeah! one Wunan." [1]

---

[1] Nyawarra, in: Jeff Doring, Gwion Gwion, p. 182 f.

2 Telboro
- Model of a Boro

Since the crucial part of the foundation of Telotopia generally lies in the Boros (or in the natural contexts of comparable forms of self-organization such as the old forms of "tribes"), the typical character of creating a Boro will be illustrated here with the example entitled "Telboro".

Specifically, Boro complexes and visuals in Telotopia definitely vary, depending on natural topography, historical portfolios (city areas and neighborhoods to be preserved) and, of course, the ideas of the respective Telotopian inhabitants. With this in mind, Telboro is not a drawing-board model according to whose numbers all other Boros in Telotopia would be built. Here, Telboro is just a model to demonstrate how the historically *in some ways* completely new structure called "Boro" is conceived.

In the shape of the "Telboro" model, we will introduce the cultural-architectural concept of Telotopia. This part, Part II, shows the external complex.

In particular, the structure called "Boro" is rooted in the development of human socialization. This is elaborated appropriately in detail in Part III.

In Telotopia, these Boros (or the tribal structures organized according to the Boros) are the normal socialization context of child development up to the twenties stage until one's own children become independent. Adults can arbitrarily choose the Boros. From the time of independence of one's own children, the further lifestyle can be arbitrarily directed, even in permanent traveling and changes of locations. But in Telotopia all this has a different foundation in society, socialization and economy than in our present society. And this is rooted in the Boro structure.

Already regarding the popular Boros, we will show that urban and natural structures can by all means be well combined, as with the old cities, even given today's population numbers. The downsides of cities as well as villages today are rooted in historical power and exploitation; they are not necessarily given as such.

2.1 On the size of population and age structure of Telboro

The size of the population number in a Boro may not exceed social manageability of a Boro. Social manageability of a Boro is the substantial foundation of overall Telotopian democratic self-regulation. However, it is not necessary for every person knowing every other person in a Boro. Manageability refers to the social processes of a Boro: to the social "effects", to "public life", and their regulation. Since the Boros are further subdivided, for example, into "settlements" and "neighborhoods", including the right to autonomy, this population size need not be that low. A population size of a Boro that is too small seems to me (beyond special natural topography) to be generally undesirable, because the cultural potential of a Boro would be too small here. A Boro is not only to manage its survival, it actually is to be a proper cultural center that matches general cultural human needs (for special needs, the "major centers", for example, are representative and available in the governing determination of the Boros, see → Part 4 for more details).

Given these considerations, I have arrived at a size of 4,000 inhabitants for a Boro (assuming an average lifespan of 80 years). With regard to a population density such as in the FRG (=Federal Republic of Germany) of approximately 231 inhabitants per km², this would mean an average Boro area of 4.16 km x 4.16 km = 17.3 km²; and at the shortest distance a path of about 4.16 km from one Boro center to the next, with more than 3 km rural territory between them. This would be equal to our present conditions in the "country", the only difference being that each Boro would actually have an urban center.

The facilities of a Boro can be quite different. These figures are only intended as a rough guide with regard to the order of magnitude presented. But they are relevant to understanding further cultural-architectural deliberations.

This size means an average year strength of 50 people. This makes up, in general, the following population structure:

Age	Number	
First year	50	
Second – third year	100	
Fourth – sixth year	150	
=	**300 infants**	
Seventh – twelfth year	**300**	= total of **600 children**

13th – 18th year	**300 adolescents**	
19th – 68th year	**2500 active adults**	
68 +	**600**	
=	**4000 inhabitants**	

So, Telboro has on average about one birth and one death per week.

2.3   The Boro concept

The organizational form of the "Boros" is the core of the concept of Telotopia. This is a certain equivalent to the former polis, an independent city-state and around for its supplies. The Boro differs, however, from the polis in that it is not absolutely independent, i.e., the right to conquests, maintaining slaves, or ecological consumption right up to ruin. It is bound to the Telotopian Constitution and is part of a worldwide federation which includes productive historical developments through to computer and space technology.

Therefore, a Boro is generally a new combination of locality, country, culture, urbanity, and state, with an average size of about 4,000 inhabitants. Each Boro is a kind of independent democratic state, but part of a federation of a worldwide organizational structure. As part of the Telotopian Constitution and other overriding rules such as those with regards to river courses, each Boro enjoys the full right to its autonomy.

The Boro is, in the first place, an organizational form that is to enable and also guarantee at the same time autonomy, such as such as a democratic definition of its broader social and economic relations that have emerged, on our planet. With this in mind, in Telotopia, the ethnological forms of "tribes" are considered and organizationally accommodated in the manner of the Boro system.

In our conditions in populated areas, however, a "Boro" as a combination of village, country, urbanity, and state at an average size of about 4,000 inhabitants is the popular common form of societal social organization.
Further organization of Telotopia is built, in stages, upon the foundation of a Boro (or, in analogous form, on "tribes"). In terms of organization, multiple Boros make up a "municipal association" (a "town or city", if necessary), multiple "districts" make up a "county", and multiple "counties" make up a "(federal) state", etc. (for more details, see → 4.4.3). It is therefore similar to today's structure. The only difference being that the higher structures are not determined by (political) parties, but consistently from below and democratically by the Boros.

For example, even "urban centers" – today's towns/cities – are formed, analogous to the "districts" and our neighborhoods, from multiple Boros (→ 4.4.2). In reverse, a Boro is also subdivided into settlements and quarters that allow one to live in autonomy and self-organization as part of a specific statute (→ 4.3.1 ff.).

So, with its only about 4,000 inhabitants, Telotopia is generally not to be misunderstood as a kind of "village life", even if its Boros offer a good village and neighborly life. Due to the comprehensive global network structure, Telotopia is able to offer all that culture, life quality as well as necessary technology that are in the positive sense feasible today.
But the initially significant fact about Telotopia is, however, its capacity to avoid all those historical downsides of independent social organization through to dictatorships, fascist systems, wars and regular break-downs of wrongly structured "advanced civilizations". The technological potential can definitely be developed into an advanced civilization – but only if the foundation of social and ecological stability is based on that which one considers culture from a human evolutionary development.

2.4 The Telboro complex
A photographic tour

The center of Telboro

From a certain perspective, the center of Telboro can be compared with the pedestrian precinct of a mid-size town, but that center is a proper "cultural center". Besides the guildhall, train station, civic hall, library and shops, this displays above all restaurants, cafés and taverns for meetings and gregariousness.

Not only is the center, but the Boros in general are generally "car-free". Everything within a Boro can be reached on foot, but bicycles can be used when necessary. The only motorized vehicles are transportation vehicles and tractors, but horses are also often used.

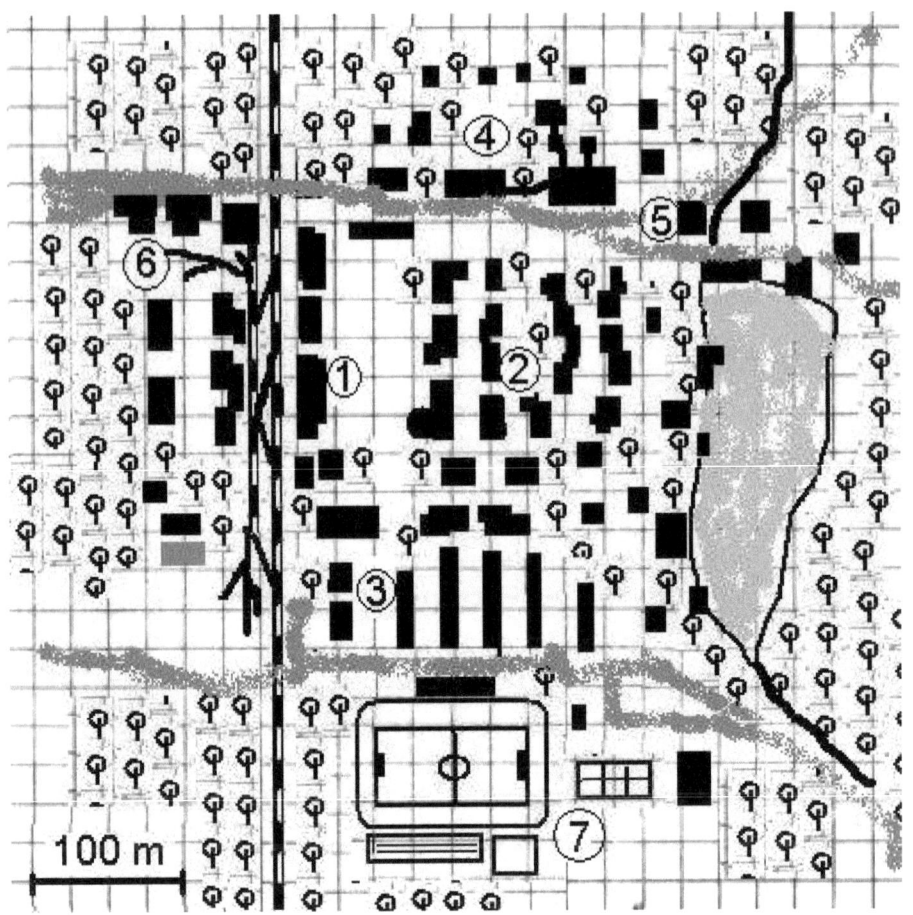

Boro map of the center of Telboro
according to the images and detailed explanations

1 Center including train station, which is at the same time the
   civic hall
2 Historic city/town center
3 Wilhelminian era quarter
4 Center of the Medical Institute
5 Facilities of the Biological Institute
6 Freight (depot) area, logistics, workshops
7 Sports center including tennis courses, stadium with tribunes,
   gymnasiums

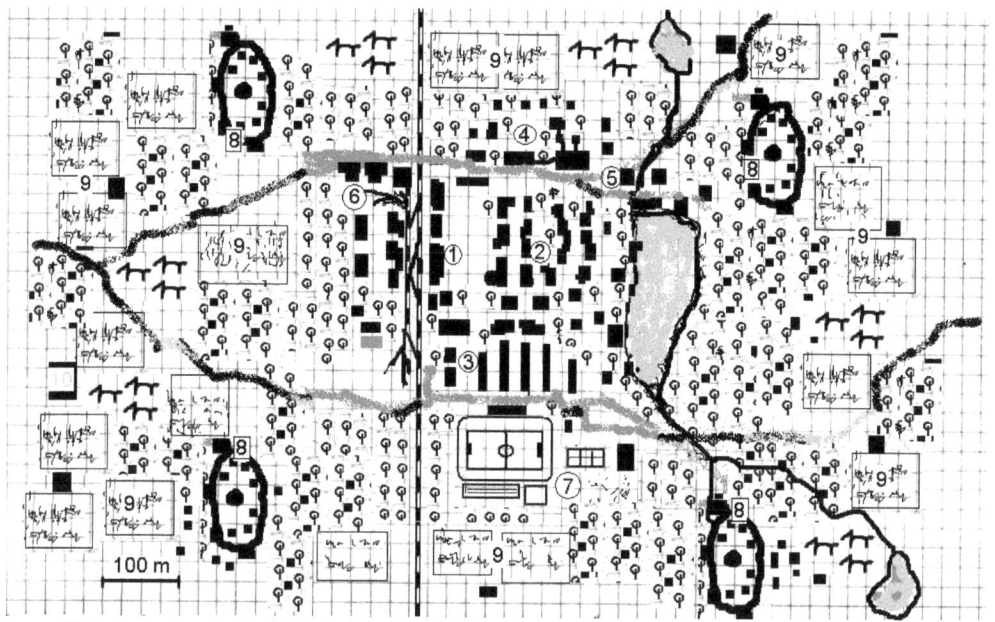

Schematized design (approx. 1200 x 800 m)

8 Transitional area of the child-garden parks (bold borders,
      with hedgerows there
9 Meadows, fields for food production (bordered)
10 Example of a farm area

The area displayed here is about 1200 x 800 meters. A Boro in which the German population density of about 231 inhabitants per km² would have to be organized, would extend about 4.16 km x 4.16 km (see below), i.e., add 1.5 km countryside in each direction, see s. → p. 176

The centers of a Boro serve social needs beyond the closer relationship life. These centers have a strong emphasis on the cultural dimension.

The Boro centers also include shops, but these are basically not independently economic, but culturally motivated. They offer what is of authentic interest according to experience. Overall, the shops are run via the Boro administration. But there are also opportunities for earning money through personal commitment.

The different character of the shops shows, already in their windows, that this is not about independent economy but about culture in its actual sense. Here, inspiring items that are also considered to be of quality are produced, but in the interest in creativity and *joie de vivre*, and not for status, privileges, etc.

Some shops will also serve, if necessary, as a meeting-place (e.g., a café) or, in certain sectors, even for production (e.g., a tailor's shop).

Design and culture are, of course, also of interest with regards to presentation and clothing. Here, too, people like to experiment in Telotopia. Overall, this area is, *from its inception*, considered under the aspect of theatrical production; at the higher level also from the eros aspect, precisely in order to avoid falling into the very gender stereotypes.

Even in Telotopia, people like ending evenings in gregarious settings. However, since the entire life there is designed from its social interest, this need not be made up in the evening. Evenings are under the auspice of ending, and this is seldom late.

The train station and civic hall of Telboro also house trade shows, theater, dancing and musical performances or also disco and dancing events.

Only the interior area of Telboro is paved (for practical reasons). To the outside are park-like areas as well as the little historic town and Wilhelminian era quarter.

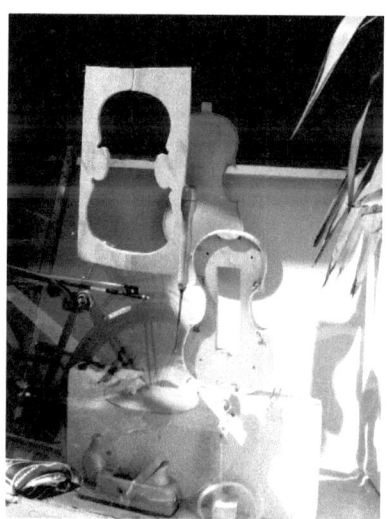

The historic town and Wilhelminian era quarter contain some small studios and production studios such as a sewing workshop, jewelry and arts & crafts workshop, violin-making workshop, etc. These can be provided by an institute for specific activities as well as for apprenticeships; they are also used as shops.

Homo sapiens has always favored setting up camp by the water. In case a Boro is not already by the water anyway, some dammed-up lakes are built, also at the edge of the center.

In Telotopia, railroad traffic plays a role, but this is rather comparable to occasional country traffic. But draisines are also frequently in use here. The corresponding train station is also used as a civic hall and as a restaurant. Behind the

For freight and people transportation, carriages are often used, which (in combination with a farm) are conducted especially by senior members and youths.

The Biological Institute

The Biological Institute plays quite a central role in each Boro. It is the central institution for on-site food production. But this significance can also be explained from the popular Telotopian interest in nature. Therefore, the Biological Institute area, situated near the center, also includes something of a zoo and museum of natural history. It also includes greenhouses with special plants not used for purposes of food (see below, e.g., cactuses). These greenhouses may also serve as cafés, teaching and learning facilities, as well as a particularly relaxed atmosphere of "being".

The different institutions (administration, teaching, production site) of the Biological Institute are preferably created ecologically in terms of their architecture and their location (use of sunlight and solar energy), but social and cultural aspects (e.g., in architecture) are always involved.

Behind the train station

If the internal center of a Boro is determined by modern insights and notions and preferably kept up-to-date, historic areas are also kept intact in Telotopia. Here, this concerns the (former) freight depot that is used for depositing, above all, as a warehouse and workshop in addition to the tracks.

The municipal area of Telboro

Adjoining to the interior center of Telboro is the historic town section and the other architectural styles of later epochs (e.g., Wilhelminian era) insofar as they are considered to be preserved and meaningful. In Telboro, this section of houses is, generally, only a rather small one and closely connected to the center; through a looser building style, it quickly sprawls into settlements and rural areas.

In the Boros, this urban building style serves only conditionally for living purposes; above all, it serves for administration, teaching, and workshops. This building style is even more pronounced in the regional centers. But the apartments there are essentially used only as a second residence, as a kind of hotel, or as a temporary stay for adults for specific activities, with children already having left home.

Behind the center (after about 100-200 meters) the actual urban building style is quite fast merging into a loose agglomeration of houses and settlements that make separate social units in a suitable structure.

That the building complex creates structured social units is an important principle of social organization of the Boros and of Telotopia in general. This is a constitutive basis for real democracy to be possible at all.

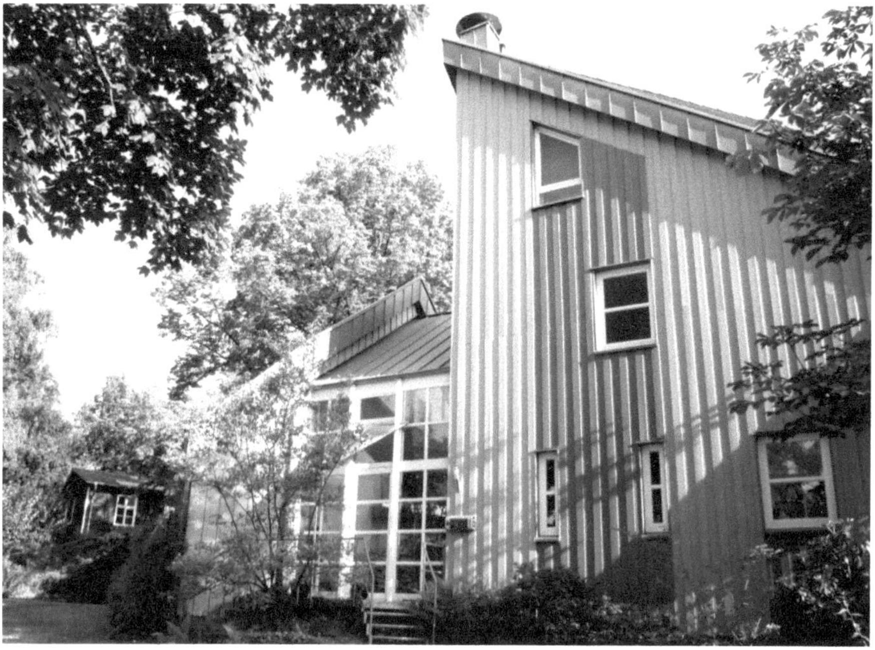

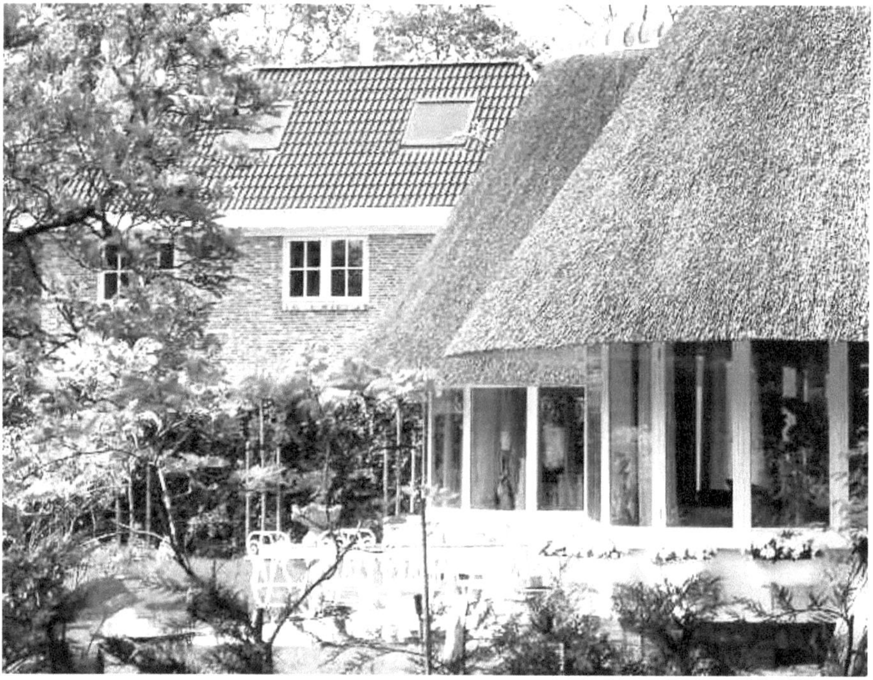

The rural area of Telboro

The rural communities and settlements are more or less connected to types of food production, e.g., even to growing vegetables in green-houses. This need not degenerate into "work". With the settlements, meals may be organized in the form of a restaurant commonly run.

Above: a household with some cultivation; below: a lumbermill (run via water power) including carpenter's shop

Living in kinds of allotment garden sites in the small settlements is quite a favorite (particularly in summer). This lifestyle is not very expensive; it offers peace and quiet, and space for artful activities, for example (even literary art). This lifestyle is also readily assumed while children are still in infancy.

Landscape picture showing a small settlement in the external area of Telboro, distance approx. 1 km;

Below: The settlement behind the lake

Besides the traditional building styles, there are many interesting forms in architecture, such as earth dwellings or tree houses. See the notes on the Internet and to literature pp. 189 and 192

3   On the Biographical Structure in Telotopia

3.1   On the significance of child-friendly conditions

The material and organizational facility of Telboro and, generally, of Telotopia, is rooted in the human disposition (anthropology, culturology) developed from human evolution and, here, initially from man's socialization evolution.

The basis of a democratic social facility that relates to man is rooted in a dialogic relationship between adults and children as well as in children-friendly conditions, as were the rule originally with camps on the beach or water places with opportunities for free play. This is based on the process logic of human evolutionary development. For the evolution of culture – as well as of creativity – has its foundation in child play, both from an evolutionary point of view and then from socialization.[2]   The significance of adults was "only" to have enabled such comprehensive childhoods and to have accommodated, appreciated and systematized the childlike impetus to culture in adult experience in social practice. In the dialogic reference between adults and children in human evolutionary development, the creative-chaotic impetus and the playful as the basis of life quality stem from childhood and social functionality and stability from adult experience.

So, insofar as one is interested in a permanent, sustained and life enjoying social life, it is impossible to avoid paying due attention to this aspect of child socialization.

With today's population numbers, a desirable culture of the future must be about evolving a cultural architectural complex that is systematically geared to the respective realities of children's needs and possibilities.

---

[2] See "A Study of the Play-Element of Culture", the subtitle of the book *Homo Ludens* by Johan Huizinga, as well as my elaborations in both my books on human evolution.

Also, creating child-friendly conditions must be understood as the basis of human rights, democracy, quality of life, and cultural level.

3.1.1 Erik H. Erikson' socialization model

The basis for the corresponding cultural architectural reflections initially is the well-known socialization model of psychologist Erik H. Erikson. Of course, this does not mean that all of Erikson's views should be adopted at a 1:1 ratio.

In this model, Erikson outlines the following eight basic stages of personality development, described in greater detail in his *Identity and the Life Cycle* (see also the chart there, pp. 178-79). For any of the items listed below, the top of the list is which development emerges in a positive case and the bottom of the list is which consequences in case of being unsuccessful may arise in the consciousness condition.

1. Trust vs. mistrust
2. Autonomy vs. shame
3. Initiative vs. guilt
4. Sense of industry vs. inferiority complex
5. Identity + rejection vs. identity diffusion
6. Intimacy + solidarity vs. isolation
7. Generativity vs. self-absorption
8. Integrity vs. despair

Of these eight stages, the first six comprise human socialization development through to reaching adulthood. Here, already the central meaning of the foundation of this evolution becomes visible in quantitative terms.

Where a successful foundation has been created here, further evolution up to the highest level, entirely according to an own authentic need, will become possible. Without such a resilient foundation, the structure of an advanced culture remains a projective imaginary product as an actual power struggle for the "top". This predestines its collapse, as can be routinely seen in previous history.

These stages of evolution of human "personality" cannot be considered in purely psychological terms. Beyond therapeutic work, this would be a silly abstraction.

In fact, these respective realities of human personality evolution must be put into practice fully in socio-cultural creation. This is the inextricable precondition for enabling the respective personality to actually direct and take command of their lives as adults by themselves. Everything else (structural violence) is an infringement against human rights.

3.1.2 The cultural architecture of the ages

What this socialization model might mean in terms of social creation with regards to social structure and education will be presented in drafts in this chapter. I do not see a complete parallel to Erikson's model here, because the perspective is somewhat different and is, above all, in the area of puberty also an issue of the respective culture.

The following model provides an overview:

Internal development according to **Erikson**	Social educational context in **Telotopia** :	
1. Trust vs. mistrust		First year
2. Autonomy vs. shame		2. + 3. year
3. Initiative vs. guilt	1) **Stage I**	Child-garden
4. Sense of industry vs. inferiority Complex	2) **Stage II**	(elementary school)
	3) **Stage III**	(from about age of 9-10)
5. Identity+ rejection vs. identity diffusion		Puberty
6. Intimacy + solidarity vs. isolation	4) **Stage IV**	Adolescence
7. Generativity vs. self-absorption	5) **Stage V**	Twenties
	6) **Stage VI**	from about 30
	7) **Stage VI**	from the 30s
	8) Individ. further education /trainings	
8. Integrity vs. despair		"Life"

The stages, in this case called "Stage I, Stage II", etc., are not, however, to be considered to be in the manner of our school classes, social classification and rating. Rather, this is about a concept of external social realities and offers of education, culture, and social contexts, to be socially reflected, equivalent to human socialization development and then to individual human personality in relation to existing requirements. This is explained in greater detail below.

3.2 Childhood

3.2.1 Infancy stage

Erikson: First stage: "I am what I am given"

"In order to ensure that their [the infants'] first experience in this world may not only keep them alive but also help them to coordinate their sensitive breathing and their metabolic and circulatory rhythms, we must see to it that we deliver to their senses stimuli as well as food in the proper intensity and at the right time; otherwise, their willingness to accept may change abruptly into diffuse defense – or into lethargy." (p. 59)

The simplest and the earliest modality is "to get", not in the sense of "go and get" but in that of receiving and accepting what is given; [...] The mutuality of relaxation thus developed is of prime importance for the first experience of friendly otherness: from psychoanalysis one receives the impression that in this *getting what is given*, and in learning to get somebody to do for him what he wishes to have done, the baby also develops the necessary groundwork to get to be the giver, to "identify" with her [the mother]. Where this mutual regulation fails, the situation falls apart into a variety of attempts to control by duress rather than by reciprocity. The baby will try to get by random activity what he cannot get by central suction; he will activate himself into exhaustion or he will find his thumb and damn the world." (p. 60)

"To look back: the first way-station was prone relaxation. The trust based on the experience that the basic mechanisms of breathing, digesting, sleeping, and so forth have a consistent and familiar relation to the foods and comforts offered gives zest to the developing ability to raise oneself to a sitting and then to a standing position." (p. 79)

I love this photo, even if some details are not (well) recognizable. It shows my grandparents in 1931 with my mother

Until the infant becomes mobile, parents in Telotopia tend to live in housing associations or small settlements outside the interior center of a Boro during the infancy stage of their children (until they are two years old). What is important is that the common type of existence with smaller children consists of an **association** of a size of about 6 to 20 adults (being the *typical anthropological social unit*).

The **decisive point** here is that each infant, from the corresponding capabilities, enjoys *independent* options of making contact and forming relationships with other children *as well as* to its parents and other familiar adults. Relations to children in Telotopia are considered a special hospitality, but never (as is the case in many previous *historical* traditions) a possession.

In view of social life in Telotopia, living with children always has other social contexts also. Couples splitting up is, beyond the personal-situational context, not a tragedy. If a couple or a single rearing person is overtaxed with handling their child, Telotopia offers plenty of opportunities for assuming this in a form best for all those involved - as attendance, support, and in various institutions offering a protected and social framework. Psychiatric problems with neurological causes can never be entirely prevented, but social ones can.

With hard conflicts regarding children appropriately trained arbiters can be involved here. In Telotopia, the priority is the welfare of children, not of adults. In case of the corresponding problems, adults have to find solutions other than absorbing children.

In Telotopia, presentation of a *problem-free spatial nearness* to other children and adults is realizing the child's human and personality rights.

Once the infant becomes mobile, a new stage begins that with regards to presenting child-friendly conditions should be considered. Housing associations in which people live may already be prepared for this. Otherwise, one would move to housing contexts that are designed for this.

The housing associations conceived for rearing infants are designed in such a manner that the infants can act independently when the corresponding options are available. Some of the adults are always nearby, either directly in the garden or, otherwise, in the house (at least one primary contact person). However, they pursue their own activities. They do not serve here as mere childminders, which does not seem to be productive. During this stage, the parents of infants pursue activities that become understandable to the children, such as gardening activities, preparing meals, certain types of needlework, and handicraft activities such as knitting, sewing/tailoring, pottery, woodwork, painting, etc. (all this stress-free and in principal openness to attending to children). These activities offer infants initial ideas about life and that's why these activities seem to impact children as equally calming as well as stimulating and promoting consciousness.

For the housing associations and small settlements designed for infant minding, horticulture is to a certain extent a widespread activity. Surplus products are either given away personally, or delivered to the corresponding places; if necessary, also exchanged for other products.

<u>Horticultural business:</u>

- cultivating vegetables: potatoes; tomatoes; zucchini (courgettes); onions; leek; cucumbers, beans, cabbages of all kinds, pumpkins, etc.,
- cultivating fruits such as strawberries, berry bushes (raspberries, etc.) and trees (apples, pears, cherries, plums, etc.)
- cultivating herbs and flowers: for decoration, out of interest in botany, for useful purposes such as sunflower seeds, for seasoning or for medical purposes.

Options of keeping small animals:
Rabbits, guinea pigs; hens, geese; sheep, goats, pigs, etc.

This may already satisfy children's "need for small animals"; maybe there are birds, dogs, cats, etc. in addition. More animals such as horses can be found in the children's and adolescents' farm sector of the child-garden and, for older children, in other sectors of the Biological Institute.

3.2.2 The child-garden parks

An example of the transition area, with a view on the contact houses

After the end of the (original evolutionary) infancy level, a new developmental stage commences about the age of three which is of significant consequence regarding external realities.

Children become decisively more independent in physical and, above all, mental terms. Erikson terms this first emerging stage as "initiative vs. guilt".

In our society, this stage is connected to sending children to kindergarten. In Telotopia, this is similar, but also decisively different. The concept of *"kindergarten"* points into the right *direction*; however, it has to be effectively rolled out.

In Telotopia, scientific insight that actual pedagogy initially consists of offering children a child-friendly living space including learning and activity options of interest to them plus the option of contact to at least one parent.

In Telotopia, this insight is realized with the park of the child-gardens. These child-gardens are a specifically larger installation of a kind of park surrounded by a hedgerow. Its facility and equipment are tailored to the needs, interests and opportunities of children aged about three to ten.

So, these child-gardens are not just created merely for the kindergarten stage (called Stage I in Telotopia), but also for developments of elementary school in our society (in Telotopia, Stage II as well as beginning and transitioning to Stage III). Out of these child-garden contexts, children can direct their own developments and learning styles in terms of speed and extent and, in the child-garden, the various offerings of play and learning are always fine-tuned to the children's interests and developments.

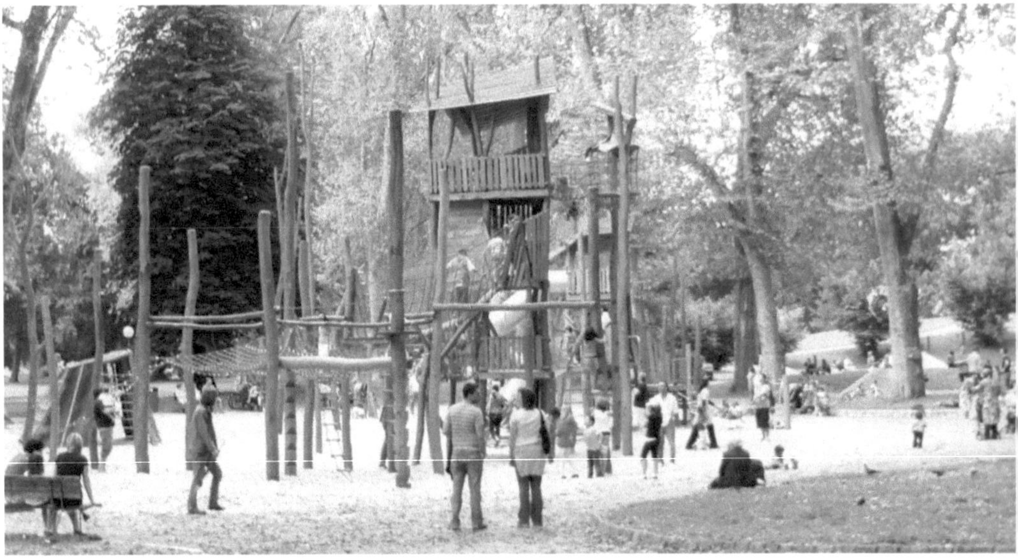

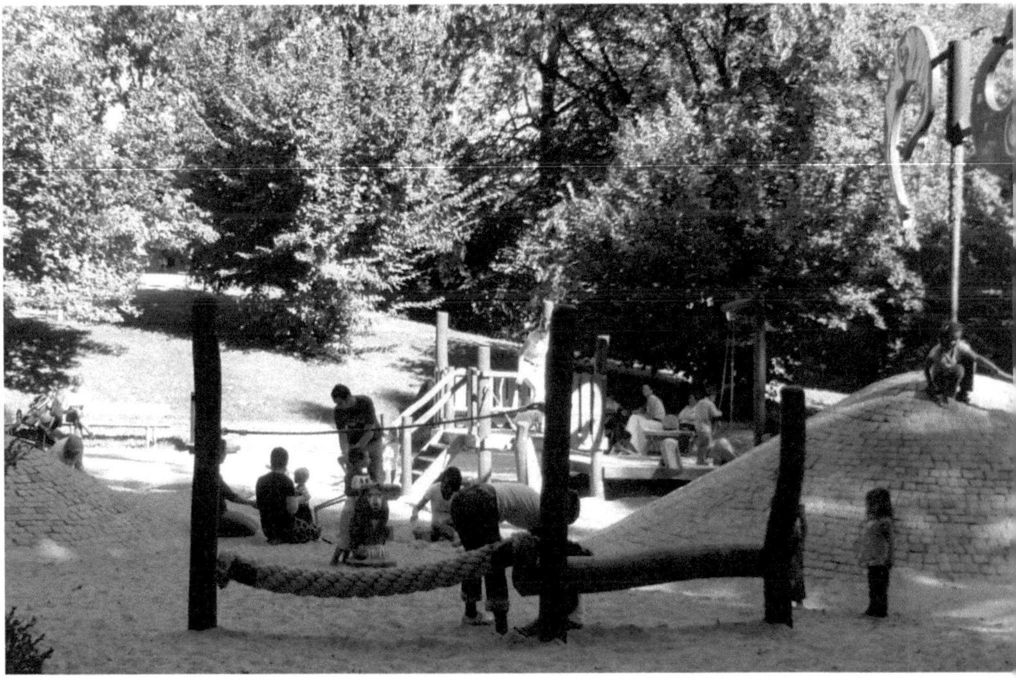

By the water (river, lake)

Overall, Telotopia's child-gardens are a park full of attractions for children and adults. It may be installed, in parts, in a "fantastic" manner like a fantasia or Disneyland. It includes a kind of circus theater with a lot of performances, narratives, playing theater, puppet shows and music; a child farm with animals and gardens; a park with various artist studios and workshops with offerings for children and adults, etc. Accordingly, it is the rule that parents also make use of these cultural offers round the corner, above all, while the children are still young. The child-garden also contains job opportunities and education offers for parents, even beyond their child context.

3.2.3 Stage I

In any event, due to the attractions for child and parents, a child already meets, prior to the age of three, a child-garden park, initially, of course, through (gradually increasing numbers of) trips.

Telboro has four such child-gardens. But overall, the number of child-gardens in Telotopia depends on the natural topography and complex of a Boro and the structure of its cultural and educational offerings.

With four child-gardens in a Boro, a year group comprises about a dozen children. For our kindergarten = Stage I, this makes - according to the year groups - 3-4 dozen, i.e., up to about 50 children and the same number again for the elementary = Stage II. Since these stages are structured, this facility is well manageable for adults, and soon will be for children as well.

Overall, a child-garden park comprises the most varied elements and institutions. These are created not just for children, they also offer parents opportunities for activities for the length of time that the children want to remain there.

This also includes washing machines and the opportunities for preparing meals, but also opportunities for career and/or cultural activities. In these child-gardens, there are also sections for horticulture and pet ownership/animal husbandry which also serve self-sufficiency. More important, however, is the colorful and varied offering, from simple being through play up to work in an autonomous mix that also make it interesting for the age of young parents to spend half a day or more there themselves, at least during the kindergarten period (Stage I).

Joining the child-garden is not compulsory for children, neither generally nor in daily life. In Telotopia, the facility of these child-gardens is "just" the generally optimal form of living connected with one's children and of enjoying something with one's children and their unique and eventually short childhood. For here the space specifically created for this is for vividness, creativity and *joie de vivre* of children and a dialogic relationship culture with children at eye level. Everyone can determine themselves in collaborative communication the, respectively, concrete design of their activities. Parents are not "childminders" here, they are not responsible for entertainment of their children and not compulsorily as the inextricable play partners. Unless parents of grandparents assume this role, pedagogues are the "childminders" in the playgrounds and devices. Parents may be together communally as they like, read a book, have a picnic on the lawn, take part in games, or pursue work and activities. At any rate, a role model should be available *independently* according to the child's need.

The structure of the child-garden parks matches the general development process of children. The playgrounds are in the entrance areas: larger sandboxes (including the corresponding toys), play equipment, lawns for picnics, lying on or playing, i.e., the area that is initially central to child development.

These are adjoined by institutions that later become interesting. Still further outside are located the specific institutions for Stage II and, all by itself at the edge and visually well protected, the institutions for very elaborate contents such as a writer's workshop, math workshop, and a "house of books" (containing books for children). There, in an attractive and relaxed atmosphere, children can be initiated by interesting people into the secrets of reading, writing, arithmetic, and life (via books), and practice them.

Overall, the child-gardens contain still further institutions, e.g., a kind of circus, a children's farm with animals, gardens and flowerbeds and vegetable patches where children can join in if they want to. All these opportunities, from playground through to circus, gardens and a "house of books", are in close proximity in the child-garden, barely more than 50 meters apart from the center to the edge. For example, children can explore these opportunities step by step in line with their development, and then use them according to their needs and interests.

So, the facility of the child-gardens and their structure adopts the new development of children commencing at the age of about three years. For this access, the playgrounds in the entrance areas are initially created.

Children start getting acquainted with the child-gardens by parents taking their child of the age of two occasionally to a child-garden. Once they realize that there is a growing interest in the child, they start to prepare themselves and their child more systematically for visiting the child-garden. First, they visit that child-garden together more frequently. When this becomes more frequent, they will look for an apartment nearby, so the child can soon go there on its own.

This is, initially, the crucial point in child development. Children are to choose their own activities by themselves and to be able to consult at least one contact person.

In any event, there are some houses available well in the proximity of the child-gardens that are suited for living with children at kindergarten age, and reserved as needed (if necessary, also specifically as a transitional period for the four-year-olds). Since there are more sophisticated and/or interesting living facilities at a negligible distance (e.g., 100 meters), people will then prefer to relocate again unless they have already moved there from the beginning. From the age of six, a path of 100 meters ore a couple of hundred meters should not be a general problem, because there are no dangers of road traffic or any other kind here.

This child will soon be able to independently go to mom or dad's workplace in the Biological Institute adjoining its surroundings

Even if the mother or parents should arrive here alone with their child, one can expect that other familiar adults will appear here with their children. Therefore, the child also has familiar playmates and for adults, too, there are most varied opportunities arising from this communal base. It would at any rate be no problem for anyone of these parents to go to one of these houses there for an hour. Even if the young child should very desperately need the respective person, there will always be a familiar adult around who can take the child to that person. Generally, after a couple of weeks, a three-year-old child is capable of orientation and, as needed, to find the workplace of the mother or father by him- or herself, given these small distances; or to master his or her way home by themselves or at least with the chosen contact person. In this way, children achieve a crucial level of independence.

Overall, a typical child-garden in Telotopia includes the following:

- a playground well equipped with sand that is located in the entrance area,

- a kind of "dredging pond", i.e., a small flat "lake" with a sandy beach for splashing and muddling; possibly, even a smaller swimming pool;

- flat terrain for playing football, for example;

- terrain with trees as an "adventure playground" for building huts, climbing, and fire pits;

- houses with kitchen and dining, play and teaching rooms;

- garden parks and a children and adolescent zoo-farm area of the Biological Institute with various animals like hamsters, ponies, etc.;

- various workshops and artist studios;

- huts or tents for circus, narrative, (puppet) show performances;

- rooms for theater plays, music, dancing, etc.

Moreover, there are typical Telotopian flexible room and roofed facilities like stretchable tarpaulins, tents, huts, and construction trailers.

(Forest kindergarten)

3.2.3.1 Creativity and games

*"Creativity first takes root
in childhood ..."* [3]

The fairy-tale uncle in
action

In addition to sound, singing and movement games, storytelling becomes important and of interest. This initially starts with fairy-tales, but increasingly, and even according to the interest of the children, it is then given a didactic logic in conveying the realities of the world.

"Very young children love and demand stories, and can understand complex matters presented as stories [...]." [4]

"Fairy-tale lessons are the highest form of teaching." [5]

"A good teacher will tell stories. [...] We are driven by *stories*, not by *facts*. Although stories contain facts, these facts relate to the stories as the skeleton does to the total human being. Anyone who thinks that learning is about swotting facts is completely wrong; details make sense only within the context, and it's this context and this sense that makes details interesting. And only when these facts are interesting with this in mind will we be able to store them." [6]

---

[3] D. Goleman, P. Kaufman & M. Ray, p. 51
[4] Oliver Sacks, *The Man Who Mistook His Wife for a Hat*, p. 174
[5] (The Germ. brain scientist) Gerald Hüther, *Was wir sind* ("What we are"), p. 164
[6] (German neurologist) Manfred Spitzer, *Lernen* ("Learning"), p. 35

Clown figures are very popular

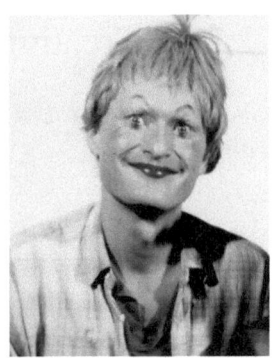

This storytelling is also offered in the shape of puppet theater and puppet shows and acting and recorded in theater-like role-playing games. As the quote from Erikson under "Initiative vs. guilt" has illustrated, the foundations of role-playing can be found in this stage. Equivalents in initial forms of theater are important here in order to create experience with regards to one's identity and one's behavioral skills. Experience in role-playing is the only safe alternative to lack of identity, false identifications, and a fixation on roles – which would not achieve the human essence of personality.

Role-playing: Re-enacting animals
Puppet show: Dolls, toy figures, dressing up; masks
Games: Dexterity exercises   Circus

3.2.4   Stage II

On this stage of "**sense of industry**" as the *alternative to developing the inferiority complex,* Erik Erikson writes:

"While all children at times need to be left alone in solitary play (or later in the company of books and radio, motion pictures and video, all of which, like the fairy tales of old, at least sometimes seem to convey what fits the needs of the infantile mind), and while all children need their hours and days of make-believe* games, they all, sooner or later, become dissatisfied and disgruntled without a sense of being useful, without a sense of being able to make things and make them well and even perfectly: this is what I call the *sense of industry.* Without this, the best entertained child soon acts exploited. It is as if he knows and his society knows that now that he is psychologically already a rudimentary parent, he must begin to be somewhat of a worker and potential provider before becoming a biological parent. [...] As he once untiringly strove to walk well, and to throw things away well, he now wants to make things well. He develops the pleasure of work completion by steady attention and preserving diligence. [...]

Third, there is the danger (probably the most common one) that throughout the long years of going to school he will never acquire the enjoyment of work and the pride of doing at least *one kind* of thing well. [...]
On the other hand, this is socially a most decisive stage: since industry involves doing things beside and with others, a first sense of *division of labor* and of *equality of opportunity* develops at this time." [7]

---

* This game is about "world of your own design" as an expression of your subject development
[7] Erik H. Erikson, *Identity and the Life Cycle,* pp. 90 - 93

When Erik H. Erikson sets the stage of **"sense of industry"**, which in his concept goes until puberty, already at the age of six years – which might well be the case –, he describes this under our conditions today as a substantial developmental stage with children.

In Telotopia, this range is not a problem because no stages of social hierarchy are connected to this. This development here commences at Stage I in the child-garden and smoothly transitions into puberty.

But given its disposition and its nature of the offer, this stage of "sense of industry", in Telotopia, must be subdivided, in terms of its level, into two principal stages: Stage II and III. Here Stage II roughly equals our (former) elementary school stage, i.e., roughly the age of six to about nine or ten, but without fixed boundaries. Stage II actually takes place in the child-garden, even if the number of trips is increasing. Whereas Stage III is, given all transitions, actually no longer part of the child-gardens; its primary form ties in with common Boro life.

Besides, even the Stage II courses themselves are not of uniform level, as our (German) grades 1, 2, 3, etc. The fundamental difference between Stage I and II is that at Stage I one is ready to see that interest is less focused on the matter and more on the playful and social aspect and that children's impetuses can definitely be erratic. If a child walks out of a Stage I painting course after five minutes, while leaving everything, this is okay. To participate in Stage II offerings requires somewhat more of factual interest and "discipline"; of course, also depending on age, on sections such as the respective stages of the courses. By and large, this does not involve any bigger problems because there is no fundamental jump from Stage I to Stage II, but the level in the courses is built step by step, according to the developmental stage of the children. If the children are considered to be mature to go to the next step, they are allowed, if they want, to take up the more advanced offering. If this is connected to changes in location and of teacher, this will be personally arranged.

Basically, the special offers of Stage II of the playgrounds, and the offers beyond Stage I can be broken into the following main sectors:

- circus – theater – handicraft/tinkering/art as the creative playful sector,

- the children's farm and household sector connected to "work", and

- the lessons sector, particularly with arithmetic, writing and reading.

Through the right conceptions, children's different levels can be accommodated, e.g., in theatrical plays when assigning scenic roles; with contributions (e.g., music/singing; juggling), and assigning tasks (like "stage construction", painting; handicrafts, including clothing). Accordingly, adults, parents and grandparents, as well as "disabled people" may be included here.

And accordingly, "art/tinkering" and "circus/theater" including games, stories, music, dancing, skill games and tinkering are the principal approaches of Stage II pedagogy of Telotopia.

"Circus/theater" may also include building huts or a section of the "adventure playground" type; in the manner of a funfair, a "market of opportunities", or even an exhibition. Besides everyday activities, special fests and, in the creative sector, exhibitions will also be organized here. This may motivate development surges and their presentations may mean special social highlights.

In this context, one can also learn how to hammer (nail), saw, or even ride horses. Many practical skills are accommodated here, or prepared in a playful way. From this, all bridges for child development can be easily built.

This holds also true with regards to the practically oriented sectors such as the children's farm and the household sector, as well as lessons in reading, writing, and arithmetic.

3.2.5   The children's farm area

In the children's farm area (no. 3 on the maps)

In our society, there is an interesting approach to children's and adolescents' farms in our child and youth work (see the ***Internet***). This approach has been accommodated in Telotopia in the shape of a children's farm sector of the child-gardens. For adolescents, Telotopia might also provide special, separate institutions, but in here these are already involved and used with the agricultural sector of a Boro through Stage III – all to the children's own needs. Adolescents can also learn how to ride horses, but horses in Telotopia also have a practical function as draft animals, rear horses, or even riding for courier services to the surrounding Boros. This combines interesting things, hobbies and practical functions with synergistic effects in a new way.

At Stage II, this is designed in a simpler form as children's farm sector in the child-gardens. The children's farm sector is organized by the local Biological Institute and it can therefore be created in a botanically and zoologically more sophisticated way, given the corresponding interest, e.g., including greenhouses, special plants, aquariums, terrariums, and maybe even some (zoo) animals. In fact, this sector may include something of a zoo. In any event, it is an attractive park to stimulate the interest of children (and even that of adults) in botany and zoology.

From the area of the Botanical Garden

This also includes basic biology lessons including animal, plant and herbal studies. As in a museum, this includes some interesting authentic material, e.g., skeletons and skulls of various animals, beautiful feathers, shells, and snail houses, fossils (maybe even a dinosaur bone), pharmacist's glasses with the most varied of contents, books and murals of herbaria that stimulate creating your own little herbaria with finds of special leaves and flowers from trips.

References to preparing food are also established here. Special berries and special fruits not normally common in the area may be available here (e.g., in the greenhouses). Certainly, special juices, smoothies, meat juices, jams and even color materials will be made here. Generally, fruits, lettuce, vegetables, herbs, and other products are available from the child-garden for daily food; these must be harvested and collected by people themselves. Not only is this very healthy. Experiencing these connections also provides a very different relationship to one's food. The wastes from food are also composted here and are therefore "disposed of" in a meaningful and even in an economic manner.

However, this children's farm sector's function is, above all, to introduce children to activities in the garden and to handling/treating animals. In doing so, an increasing number of opportunities are offered, if interested, corresponding to the sense of industry, of joining the work, or of planting your own small beds. For some parents, this sector is a real workplace.

Of course, this work in the gardens can be distributed in an easy-going manner. If necessary, people go to their patch in the morning, watering the plants as needed, realizing and discussing the work to be done. Even the scope of work is by arrangement. Even for adults, work will hardly make up more than four to five hours spread over a day. Perhaps people work for just one hour per day, however, or even just as occasional assistants with special requirements (such as in spring when preparing beds).

Actually, the local Biological Institute is responsible for organization in the children's farm sector. But since children are generally interested in various activities in the children's farm sector, there are normally no problems with the activities – the exception perhaps being extraordinarily lasting bad weather (beyond the winter season) where children lose interest here. Of course, minor natural disasters such as heavy rain can mess up the usual work process for the current year. However, this will not keep children from joining again the next year.

Farm holidays. At the age of 9, I (center) enjoyed helping farm workers with harvesting potatoes and loading hay (photo).

3.2.6   Stage III

Stage III here means the higher level of the "sense of industry" stage, stretching, via a broad transitional phase, into puberty. This would equal approximately the age of 10 to 14/16. The beginning of sexual maturity, however, depends on culture and conditions. In Telotopia, that beginning might therefore start (again) later in favor of the playful stage, but this is not really significant here.

The beginning of Stage III emerges from the extension of Stage II. It still starts with the child-garden phase, but the actual step to Stage III might also be marked by a site outside the child-garden. Since developments here are, according to the authentic state of the children, created in a smooth transition phase, both might be the case at the same time, depending on the children's interest. A Stage II child, interested in specific aspects, may attend Stage III courses, just as a Stage III child may still feel rooted in the child-garden, if necessary, also as an educator to younger children.

A specific institution of the Biological Institute of Telboro is considered as a special Stage III site. This is located near a child-garden and at the intersection between the Boro center and the external section. It serves as a special link between various sections developed in Stage III. In the first place, this serves as a social framework for Stage III learners, as a specific meeting place where they may also prepare a common meal (if necessary, using self-harvested produce) and eat it together and where space for certain separate learning exercises in the manner of our homework (but autonomous) is available.

Overall, Stage III might be called a certain precursor of internships, training courses and studying, but without tearing up the relation to the child-garden, the playful, and the creative. All forms of Stage III are considered to be offerings and suggestions and very much as agreement with Stage III learners.

If the weather is good enough for this, the corresponding trips are made with Stage III learners after the morning meeting: in worse weather conditions to the interiors of the Biological Institute, for example, to workshops, factories and institutions of the center; in good weather, to the nature areas of the Boro, to the agricultural factories and some peripheral settlements. Initially, this also obtains simply for the purpose of physical activity. All this will then be increasingly taken to a higher level.

Initially, trips into nature are frequently combined with games, e.g., a "scavenger hunt" (where the leading group has to leave certain signs and the following group must track the leading group) or a competition where certain tasks have to be solved at specific "stages" until you are allowed to proceed to the next stage, etc.

During "excursions", many realities of nature will be introduced. One is now being acquainted with all sorts of trees, shrubs, herbs, etc. One creates a herbarium, for example, where one archives dried leaves, blossoms, and herbs. Here one can then learn which herbs are edible, can be enjoyed as teas, and are usable as seasoning and healing herbs. At a higher level, one may also learn what a specific growth says about the soil and climate and what are the overall biotope relationships in the different areas, etc.

The sports facilities of Telboro can be sought out for specific physical activities (beyond the child-garden). This includes external sections for athletics and matches like football, beachball, hockey, tennis, etc., and internal sections for gymnastics, climbing and indoor matches like (badminton), table tennis, handball, volleyball, etc. A certain physical activity may be assumed as a natural need of humans and also of children, for Man as a "biped" by nature is specifically designed to mobility. Telotopia does not have the schizophrenic phenomenon of preaching "exercise, exercise" but condemning humans from a very young age on to basically sit at home and at school (which actually does have some reasons but is derived basically from a badly designed culture).

Telotopia also includes sports contests and it is even recommended to test your physical boundaries, but in Telotopia this is seen from an approach towards affirming one's body and feelings. There is no sense of performance sports and over-emphasizing competitive features. There will be football and other clubs, but in the manner of our amateurs. In Telotopia, there is no profit in sports. However, bicycle tours and travel around the world would be possible and one could pursue the corresponding hobbies in this scope in combination with other activities when interested. For example, activities as a sports teacher, fitness coach (e.g., also in the therapeutic, rehabilitation and seniors sectors), bicycle courier (even including trolleys), touristic sector, as an "adventurer" (in combination with journalistic activities), as a climber in research contexts, and in the repair sector with high-rise buildings, etc. would be conceivable in this context.

After the basic introductions into Stage III, the individual sectors will be given more attention. Most Boro workshops include dates at which Stage III learners (if necessary, initially in groups) make a visit and can watch the activities. When interested, Stage III learners can then go into a kind of internship. This generally starts initially small-scale, e.g., through a shorter phase of one hour per day. With a pronounced interest and the corresponding opportunities, this can also be designed more extensively. Overall, however, Telotopia's orientation is that Stage III learners first are acquainted with all sorts of things, building up a preferably extensive horizon. The educational program of Stage III is geared towards this.

This approach is also met through spatial extension of excursions. It goes more and more beyond trips beyond the Boros. This relates to all orientations: in matters of nature, trips to mountains, for example, a voyage, or hiking in special landscapes; trips to specific museums, castles or even leisure parks (e.g., even together with the family); relating to specific functional interests, visits to interesting production facilities and (presumably, however, more from puberty on) urban functional centers (town facilities such as historic towns, accumulation of special shops).

A trip to a lake or to the sea

These trips are also pedagogically used very specifically in order to counter premature fixations on specific activities and its Boros. Interest in the world is also to be kept up beyond the Boro (which the original cultures of Homo sapiens were able to cherish through their relatively free migrations). Telotopia needs the Boros to prevent losing the social and democratic ground in anonymous and abstract social conditions. But the Boros need connections to the world beyond their Boro to prevent degenerating into petty-mindedness and restrictions. This horizon is built at Stage III.

In practical terms, however, the priority of Stage III developments is initially on the agricultural sector and procurement of food. This is a sector that corresponds to understanding, hands-on options, as well as various interests of Stage III learners (always autonomous, however).

What begins in initial form in Stage II will be taken to a higher level in Stage III. Here one learns how to create gardens and to cultivate plants and, if possible, also how to keep small animals.

Keeping animals includes some further aspects here. In our area this will touch on particularly to keeping horses which should generally be relatively widespread in the Boros, where horses will continue to be used as draft animals, even back horses in forestry. But they should also be of some interest as riding horses to children and adolescents.

Last but not least, horses are, above all, used as always for preparing Stage III learners for the topics of maintenance and relationship. These mammals have, in terms of bone structure and internal organs, a major equivalent to the human body. In this way, biology can prepare for a lot of medical knowledge without including this not merely simple relation from the start. Initially, one may be properly amazed at the fantastic range of the "wonder of life", about the versatility of plants and animals, about the complexity of their planting, about the contexts of life and habitats, and via the commonalities that do exist in spite of all differences (such as "cells" with plants and animals).

It's a good idea to build an extensive horizon even in this respect before the Big Topic of Life displays its actual impact upon Stage III learners: finiteness and the limits of life and one's self. Life and real love are not harmless. Of course, one may content oneself with a "tut-tut" attitude. But this does not make any sense for Telotopia. Social life at this level does not have any viability; it does not work in truly autonomous social conditions either. In a Boro, this would be immediately visible.

3.3 Puberty and adolescence

Puberty is not actually about sexual maturity, but about a new moratorium, triggered by the beginning of sexual maturity, to develop one's ability to self-regulation (=>"identity" or "self"). This new moratorium emerged following the older hominid moratorium of "sense of industry" in the human evolutionary development as the consequence of severing from the genetic behavioral control of the animal stage.

Whereas with animals sexual maturity immediately establishes adult status merging into parenthood, the human evolutionary moratorium establishes the completely new human dimension of "personality" and "culture". Unlike the animal stage, personality is itself no longer determined through the position of social hierarchy (e.g., "alpha animal") but in the capability of self-regulation and communication as in the new human ability to relate and deal with conflict. As the length of the moratorium between sexual maturity and adulthood proves, this cannot be achieved in passing. In fact, this stage should be considered the actual human evolutionary development from animal to human and, from an evolutionary standpoint in its entire phase, it has emerged for evolving that which it is about concerning Man with personality and culture. Therefore, we shouldn't be surprised in the least that if this crucial human development is neglected a bungling social life and behavior including power, competitive behavior, violence and wars emerges – where the hominids already fell prey to extinction with all their sense of industry and their technological intelligence.

Specifically, understanding the processes of this moratorium, of the terminology ("puberty", "adolescence", "autonomy", "maturity", etc.), of their design and even the physical development connected with them depended on the respective culture. How "adulthood" (socially and legally) is defined is also dependent on what support an individual gets from their social contexts and which responsibility that individual is burdened with through which consequences.

In Stage III, activities and trips are getting more frequent and extensive anyway. In this form, the more specific moments of puberty are also accommodated.

These trips, which are conducted under the direction of specially seasoned pedagogues, serve to support the growing adolescents in detaching from their parents and enabling them to display their own responsible behavior, which largely renders the conflicts that exist in our society superfluous.

In Telotopia, the area of sexuality, fertility and offspring are actively accommodated from scratch, of course, in a didactically reflected manner. Children know already from a very young age that there are males and females, girls and boys (according to my own experience, [sometimes?] from a very early age). Due to the personality development in Telotopia, the historic problem of inhibitions and overreactions regarding nudity and sexuality is non-existent (at least not to this high degree).

In Stage III, this topic arises, as in earlier ages, very naturally in the context of farming and livestock breeding. In Telotopia, understanding reproduction is taught in this context, perhaps initially with special regard to plants, but also with regard to animals. Without specifically taking human realities into account here, this area is didactically and consciously included here. Taking the bodies of animals and, above all, those of mammals like dogs, sheep, cows, horses, etc., it is shown that the female body features tits for feeding the offspring and a womb in which the offspring grows, and that the male body has testicles and a penis, which serve insemination. This system is widespread in nature, and through conveying this the human fact merges with a more general view of biology.

Based on this, specifically human issues can then be linked quite differently to the personality level, confronting one's feelings and needs and communication as the crucial basis of human relationship conditions.

In this context, there is no need for gender stereotyping – on the contrary, this is considered in Telotopia as an obstacle to developing personality and genuine, i.e., personal, relationships. In Telotopia, the sensational aspect of sexuality is not rooted in genitalia and sexual intercourse with preferably high-ranking ("attractive") sexual partners, but with love and (irreplaceable =) personal relationships.

Thus, the question of coeducation in this area is obsolete in Telotopia. In Telotopia there will be offers that are aimed more at the interests of girls as there are those aimed more at the interests of boys. Some of it can be offered "for girls only" and "for boys only", as well as for mixed groups. The prospective adolescents will make up their own minds as to what they want. It will be assumed here that, above all, with the rise of sexual maturity certain different interests exist as well as the need to initially digest one's physical changes and new questions by oneself. But this need not to be determined from "above". The offerings should go in those different directions and the prospective adolescents will see for themselves what they think is best for them.

To give but one example here. For boys, special "adventure" trips might be of interest here, e.g., an expedition through a (non-touristy) cave, or even including a (correspondingly staged) "dragon fight", etc. For girls, trips to special horse farms including horse-riding opportunities might be of special interest. This also includes the motive of partnership and is, of course, also connected to an interesting peek "under the belly". Perhaps specific courses in the nursing sector, if necessary, even in the context of births and babies, will be offered here.

Furthermore, there are special courses in encounters between the sexes. It does not seem to be insignificant to guide the beginnings in this process and to convey notions of usable manners.[*]

---

[*] In this I see a reason for the emergence of and in the stock of historical barbarism (in decaying social life and the emergence of power, possessions, and patriarchy, etc.) in that the original learning and educational process, originally linked to puberty, decayed at the end of the Ice Age and that for the purpose of tribal or clan alliances the offspring was used for a marriage policy. Out of this practice the idea of animal husbandry also emerged which impacted in reverse as neolithic domestication pedagogy.

A tried and tested form is linked with dancing. This may start at first with given patterns, and then transition into more autonomous forms of interaction. Qualified work with forms of theater provides optimal opportunities. Well-tailored roles can help adolescents to enunciate and present themselves. Following this, performances of suitable encounters and relationships can then be started where actual performances should exist in Telotopia. Adolescents can then continue this with their own designs. In doing so, they can experiment with behavioral forms, and learn how to reflect and communicate via their own performances.

Because in reality it is not nudity and sexuality that are the problem and central theme, but understanding one's actual needs within the complexity of dealing with potential partners. Nothing requires more of identity and ability to deal with conflict than Eros love. But where the ability to deal with conflict and the ability to love have been acquired, the foundation for transforming negative tensions of competitive and power fights into a positive and intriguing social and relationship life. This is exactly wherein lay the secret of success of the human evolutionary development into Homo sapiens.

For further questions regarding conveying sexuality to adolescents, Telotopia will provide qualified sexuality pedagogues who are not just biologically informed but who themselves also understand love and relationships.

"Love is not primarily a relationship to a specific person; it is an attitude, and orientation of character which determines the relatedness of a person to the world as a whole, not towards one 'object' of love."

Erich Fromm, The Art of Loving, p. 43)

3.3.1 Stage IV

Overall, the Stage IV is, at any rate, significant for social and cultural learning in developing one's personality and one's relationship and social contexts.

Experiments in living in a hut settlement play a particular role here. Initially, this is not yet about living permanently in a hut settlement. Generally, it starts just as with a trip, with tents and huts, maybe initially for two weeks. This might be continuing a trip where perhaps a specially good commonality feeling has evolved. This special experience beyond ordinary everyday life is now transformed back into the Boro's known everyday life in order to detach from childhood socialization. This is to impart in particular that one's very **own** life context in everyday life is the space to recognize, test and actualize one's own ideas, notions and imaginations of life.

The task of the lecturers who at the beginning are partially immediately present in the hut settlement is to accommodate juvenile experiences in a new and separately emerging "world" and to strengthen the processes of communication and reflection. What sort of forms of living, social processes, activities, and forms of housing would be desirable for them? Which experience is available in this regard from previous history?

This analysis is now "put into practice". After the first course of, say, fortnightly hut living in one's own Boro, the next course will be planned. Perhaps some of the participants did not like it and will not take part in the next experiment in this combination. Or perhaps there are other adolescents from the Boro (or perhaps from a neighboring Boro with contacts) who want to join the next time. Or perhaps they want to try out another site or (better) prepare one thing or another for next time. Immediate proximity to one's home context makes some things more possible, and better.

An important issue in these courses with experiments in the hut settlements will be architecture, setup and obviously also building a larger or smaller hut. Perhaps an existing hut will be redesigned or a tree house, tiny or earth house be built; a village as a fort or castle with towers (see designs by Austrian artist Hundertwasser).

Even living in trailers or discarded wagons at the back of the freight depot is occasionally tested.

In Telboro, this hut life, increasing during Stage IV, is the starting-point for conveying effective independence and awareness in all areas of one's livelihood there.

This starts with building furniture, pottery work, tailoring, cooking, horticulture, etc. The goal here, however, is not genuine autarky, which some people might take up as a (temporary) goal, though. It's more about getting an idea of all the elements of one's livelihood. This makes one systematically more capable of deliberately fashioning one's own life and to comprehend one's social life and to learn how to communicate. This will soon become of interest to Stage V when through one's offspring a temporary fixation of one's now independent social and relationship life emerges. To be initially qualified as well as possible for this is the central special meaning of Stave IV and the possible experiments with an independent hut life.

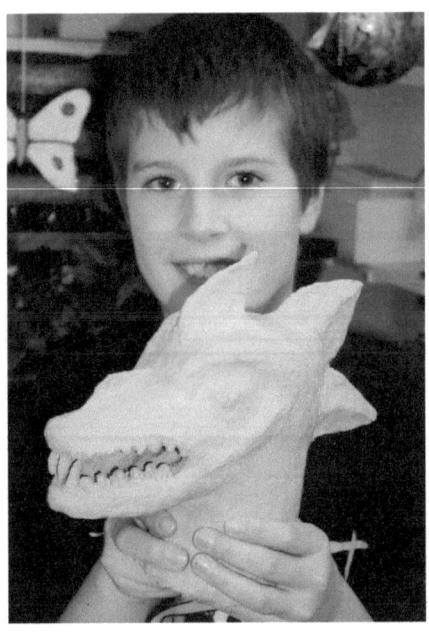

Author's hobby products including pedagogic support

120

3.4 Adulthood

3.4.1 Stage V

Very generally, Stage V is the stage for the twenties age group. In terms of its step from Stage IV, it corresponds to the "Generativity vs. self-absorption" stage in Erikson's model.

More pronouncedly, two generally different dimensions are linked with Stage V: on the one hand, a stage of personality development: the beginning of effective adulthood – and, on the other hand, a stage in the sector of education and training, studies, and regarding activities. Correspondingly, Stage V may perfectly mean different things in the most varied of sectors.

In particular, however, Stage V is the stage of births and rearing young children. Women may, according to desire, bear children sooner or later (later, for example, in cases where a child died still during childhood and therefore the right to a "new" child exists). In general, however, Stage V in Telotopia is biologically, culturally, and also biographically ideal for the desire to have children.

One does not miss anything in Telotopia when devoting oneself to one's children in the first place, particularly during the infancy stage: nothing social, no educational or vocational opportunities and, above all, nothing of a quality of life. No one will be isolated here because of children. Experiencing one's children's growth is considered to be exciting and a special opportunity in life here; in Telotopia, at this age people are closer to the simple life of children. More sophisticated studies, researches, travels and vocational activities can still be taken on when interested – in Telotopia, this would be generally in one's thirties and there would still be enough life time, both on a personal and a social level.

Those with notions of special objectives early on in their lives may also prepare for this, in the most varied of forms, already during their twenties (courses in the Boro, practical activities, remote study, etc.).

But nobody is compelled here to do it in this way. This only obtains here generally as favorable and as an average, but is not therefore considered to be normative: because the actual individual is, regarding personality development, the uppermost entity of Telotopia. Those who feel connected to very specific things early on (e.g., a musician with a high level of skill, etc.) may take a different path early on. Educational levels in Telotopia are age-related only in terms of their tendency, but not in absolute terms. Concerning certain specializations, one might join Stage III at an early stage and end up in Stage VI in quick succession, which in our society corresponds to a study course at university. As with us, one might be in a full-time job early on and enter parenthood only in one's thirties or even forties. But this should not be frequently the case in Telotopia, though it would be perfectly fine. Only, these exceptions would not be considered the rule in Telotopia and the corresponding tendencies are, in our society, also connected to our emergency conditions because the economic and therefore a corresponding economic situation come first.

In Telotopia, life can be lived in a relaxed manner in every respect. Here, one has sufficient time for one's life, for one's individual development, for one's children as well as for one's relationships. From this, the stage according to Erikson's Stage VI = Stage V suggests itself for the time of having and raising children.

3.4.2 Adult life beyond parenthood

During the latter part of the twenties, a different relation to life emerges piecemeal. Previously life was shaped by socialization development where, step by step, new things entered one's horizon of consciousness, latterly via any prospective children of one's own.

When those prospective children of one's own are now starting, in the context of Stage I, to develop a certain independence, a new life stage also emerges for their parents. Perhaps they already have specific ideas as to what they want to get out of life. Or perhaps they are sufficiently content with the realities to allow the rest of their life happen to them. At any rate, there is still plenty of time here for living one's life and Telotopia offers all sorts of opportunities for this. Let's take the age of 28 here, then you have a full 40 years ahead of you until you enter the age stage at 68. There is no economic pressure here. You don't need to hurry here either to grab attractive jobs and positions. In Telotopia, such an attitude would be considered not to be positive, but a problem of lack of maturity.

As long as one's own children have not reached the stage beyond puberty, this situation is taken as one's own premiss in Telotopia anyway. Long journeys spanning many months, or remote activities would be taken on only after that period. There are still enough opportunities for that.

What is initially frequently linked to this age stage in Telotopia is an interest in one's ongoing development. This can take many different forms: It can simply consist of taking more time for oneself and one's interests beyond the children, or even to devote oneself more to one's already existing relationships, social contexts and/or activities. However, it may also consist in taking on a more sophisticated activity or further education/training at Stage VI level.

3.4.3 Stage VI

In terms of content level, Stage VI as a Telotopian educational stage corresponds approximately to that which is designed as a course of study with higher education and corresponding activities. Transitions to Stage V are fluid. It would be well conceivable that parts of university studies (in our society) are designed as Stage V, but in a more easy-going form. Stage VI would then (in parts) equal the final stage of studying, the Master degree, and then even graduation.

Popular life in a Boro does not require Stage VI education and this makes even only limited sense as part of a permanent life in a Boro. To whom living permanently at Boro level is desirable, the quality of life will actually be found on levels other than the Stage VI forms, or they might accommodate the Stage VI offerings just in parts as hobbies. This is also absolutely legitimate in Telotopia; it is quite widespread there, because there is lively mental activity.

Though Telotopia is, to a certain extent, dependent on there being enough people interested in activities, via the precondition of Stage VI, in studies and education/training. In some medical areas and for some technologies like computing (and space research), this remains essential. But if interest in the Stage VI sector in Telotopia should be only very low, this would not be an actual deficiency. Overall, there is no necessity for a high level in this sector. Furthermore, as in our society, specific jobs are connected to specific remuneration. In Telotopia, those who are genuinely interested in living at a sophisticated level can achieve this via specific activities. In Telotopia, however, attention is paid to the fact that this is part of the authentic. Imposture stands no chance here. Also, land and houses can never become a property, and are not heritable either.

In relation to our society today, the Stage VI sector is absolutely necessary for organization of Telotopia only to a fairly limited extent. However, it is to be assumed that, as with our society, there is a greater interest in it. As little as can be said against finding life in a Boro (or even a simple monastery facility within this) completely satisfactory, so it should be assumed that there are a number of people to whom tapping into some of the higher technical and cultural potential that has emerged will appeal from a quite authentic perspective. Only, in Telotopia this will be aligned to ecological sustainability and social quality of life rather than in economic and power political expansive form. As much as this interest exists, the corresponding institutions will be created in Telotopia.

Since in Telotopia the Stage VI level does not result from biographical competition for privileged careers and positions but from authentic personality development, at the general level this does not start already at the end of the teenage years. As such this should be well possible with a corresponding qualification (entrance exams) and the Stage V sector, too, can also achieve a high level when people are interested. But generally, the Stage VI level will be taken in its fullest form only from the age of 30, when one's children have reached a certain level of independence during Stage II, or eventually only after their puberty stage.

At first glance, this appears to be quite late. Stage VI does not start from zero, however. Our relation between school and university does not exist here. Rather, it equals the field of doctoral theses and assistant jobs. So, the notion that this age would be too late for a higher mental and practical level has no basis at all. Most of all, from your personality development, you contribute a different level in understanding the technical aspects and in appropriating the subject material.

Attendance in Stage VI courses is regulated, as always in Telotopia, through fulfilling the entry requirements. As always, the degree of development and temporal distribution and length remain autonomous. There are no "semesters" here. The courses may take hours, days, weeks, months, and years.

You will always see how the courses are working – from the situation, the realities and from group dynamics, and you will draw the corresponding conclusions. Maybe a completely different result is the outcome instead of the originally conceived one, but even this will be considered good, because it is based on authentic process logic here.

Of course, certain qualifications may be necessary in order to attend other courses or to take on corresponding activities, but this is an effectively internal logic here. Without these qualifications, the new subject material will not be understood and the respectively set tasks cannot be fulfilled. You don't want to be medically treated by anyone not sufficiently qualified to do this job. You don't want course teachers who are not really up to their subject, nor do you want any insufficiently qualified managers or Boro representatives. This is always about an equivalent to the respective functions, nothing else.

Perhaps Stage VI should quite soon be extended to Stage VII, for example, where the latter boils down to what we, to a certain extent, associate with the graduate level and other faculties for highly qualified research and activity fields. How the relationship between the one and the other should be defined more precisely is pointless here. There will in any case be an entire range, which will be very different depending on faculty and a concrete position.

In Telotopia, finding out your own logic is part of studying itself. You can't win or lose a status here. You study for interest in contents and/or for the purpose of qualifying for activities that you consider to be corresponding to your personality in some way, or at least try this from this perspective.

This is the same as it's fine for one person to hike through mountains in ordinary tourist manner (because other things are also of importance), while others feel climbing the Matterhorn in Switzerland or Mount Everest to be their challenges.

It's a matter of the respective personality. Making too few demands is just as much a problem as making too many demands. This is to be avoided in Telotopia. Telotopian culture is oriented towards the equivalent to the respective personalities because in this is realized the optimum equally for individual personalities as for society and one's culture. Both ordinary mountain trips and climbing Mount Everest mean "life" insofar as this is the – current – equivalent of personality and both will be made possible only through a workable social federation. Hiking in the Sussex Downs or the Appalachians, etc. is not such a sensation; however, it does not take so much effort and therefore enables other things. Whereas climbing Mount Everest is a completely different experience which also claims significantly more energy, risks, and resources. The bottom line is that this balances out in Telotopia's understanding. Orientation there is not related to individual items but to actualizing life, personalities and permanently good social conditions that become possible through the equivalent to the respective personalities.

Thus, the benefit for a head physician in Telotopia eventually is exclusively in that his much more specific interest will be promoted and in that he can take on a very special task. Motivation to become head physician in order to impress or to make big money does not stand a chance in Telotopia. Nobody there would consider such a personal status to be particularly trustworthy or qualified (at the latest, not at university). From the viewpoint of Telotopia, a head physician does not perform more than a nurse or a charwoman or an angler; they just perform "different things", *everything* of which is believed to be good, important, and to be acknowledged. The differences here are based solely on the personality traits themselves. Telotopia's social contract is that you strive to enable each other to match your personality, regardless of whether it is simple or demanding. Whatever becomes possible here, it is the real possible optimum. It won't be 100% of the desirable, but that's only possible in "heaven". Where one is adult, one will reach an adult ratio regarding cutbacks. At any rate, the cutbacks here are not rooted in socially degenerate conditions and the correspondingly oriented personality structures.

For example, on the one hand one will work towards achieving one's dreams and, on the other, towards liberating oneself from the fixations on them.

In Telotopia, the appeal to study and to master challenging tasks is in the respective thing itself and therefore rooted in the personality. In this respect, there is (except in emergencies) no hurry, apart from personal interest. The effectively human substance on which social life can build is, however, in these facts. Antisocial motivations of "enforcement" and "high posts" do not stand a chance here. Such weird personality forms would inevitably be noticed by the teachers and other participants in the university courses. Of course, each adult in Telotopia knows that everyone has their limits and their defects and this is completely recognized. Only, these limits and defects may not disrupt execution of the respective offices and activities. But these would be aspects that would be accommodated in time during education/training at the latest, if not already during childhood, e.g., through playing theater, etc.

There are, accordingly, "filters" in the educational courses of Telotopia, because it is never the thing itself, but always social life and the personality level that are always in focus. The course directors would accommodate it in all sorts of areas as an issue if behavior is "inadequate" as ends and means. Each person would be made to understand that they would not do themselves a favor when the respective aims are too high or wrongly motivated, just as in reverse there would be encouragement for more when more potential is recognizable with a person: but this would be from an interest in that person.

At any rate, an entire system of "filters" prevents socially relevant offices to be taken by factually or socially and humanly unsuitable persons. In Telotopia, those who want to become "king or queen" are given enough opportunities in the theater arena, but not in the political or technological arena. Everyone makes mistakes at some point, but in Telotopia there is no particular reason, *due to these filters in the trainings*, to encounter the personalities in the higher political administrative posts with mistrust, anymore than a head physician.

3.4.4   Living one's life

You don't have to study, travel to remote countries, take on special hobbies such as sailing, surfing, skiing, etc. Pure (co-)living in a Boro in itself offers enough quality of life. Whether traveling, specific activities and jobs mean, respectively, happiness or stress, value, or problem is not due to the things in themselves but to their equivalent to personality, their situation, as well as to the social conditions.

The crucial point is to obtain, ever more precisely, further and more consciously, access to oneself (one's self), one's feelings, one's relationships and conditions and to learn how to actualize this as actual "life". In this way, one will reach increasing quality of life, at the same time socially and socio-culturally, wherein is the real wealth.

> "Anyone who does something for love will get their due through their action, because they lend expression to a lively feeling, actualizing themselves. Anyone who does something out of conformity or relinquishes something that might hurt someone else opens up an inner calculation that binds them to the past and the future, but largely deprives them of the present." [8]

In Telotopia, more and more options are opening up with increasing age. What has been learned has been learned, what has been developed has been developed. If you defer a trained activity in favor of new activities for a time, then you may no longer be that fit in it, but you will be able to catch up pretty soon.

---

[8] Wolfgang Schmidbauer, *Die Angst vor Nähe* ("The Fear of Intimacy"), p. 68

With long-time relationships, it does not matter when you do not see each other for a year because of traveling or when you see each other only occasionally because you are commuting between Telboro and a functional center due to studying or a job. In this way, the experience adds up to an ever-increasing wealth and here Telotopia offers you, even at 40, an average of still another 30 or even 40 years ahead of you.

It's pointless to list and go through all the possibilities in their various courses, because they are very specifically linked with a "personality" and one's "consciousness".

Overall, I see some six areas here that play a role with regards to shaping a quality of life:

1. **"Being"**
2. **Hobbies, cultural matters**
3. **Traveling, hiking, sports**
4. **Study, research, further education/training**
5. **Activities**
6. **Relationships**

Here are some keywords   :

1. "Being"
simply living one's life and taking part in social life
considered in spiritual terms: meditation, convent
life, pilgrimages

2. Hobbies, cultural matters
Sports; travel, hiking; climbing, mountain tours
Art; dancing; music; theater
cooking; handicraft/tinkering;
Voluntary work; care services;
Studying, researching; correspondences

3. Traveling, hiking, sports

Visiting various countries, cultures, areas
Hiking or bicycle trips around the world; horse-riding

Train journeys, voyages (sailing, etc.)
in old age + for the disabled: using specific trains, and
Ships and escort.

5. Activities

in particular, medicine, high-tech; coordination work

6. Relationships

Children, parents; love, friendships; communities

In particular, I'm interested in what is possible as part of a two-per-
son relationship.

"Fairy-tales told at campfires, complex sand sculptures and dancing representing the myths of the group, all these leave no traces. But it is these that are the essence of being human of hunter-gatherer societies." [9]

"But what induced man, all over the globe, to artistic activity on such a scale? The immense scope of already existing documentation shows cave paintings and rock art as a global phenomenon that makes up, in terms of quantity, over 90 percent of known prehistoric representations. Rock art [...] begins with *Homo sapiens* [...].
One wonders what induced man to imprint the signs of their visual creativity everywhere. It seems as if this is a kind of fourth dimension of the explorer spirit that not only seeks to discover the world surrounding him but also seeks to understand the existential relationship of man to nature and the world.

In view of mile-long galleries with rock engravings and thousands of images as can be found in various areas of the Siberian tundra the question arises as to who were the artists who created these works. It was probably small groups that over generations returned to the same locations to perform the same actions here. Apart from their art, they hardly left anything, at best some hut floors, relics of fire pits, some rudimentary tools. These sparse relics of those activities, which were necessary for economic and physical survival, stand in contrast to their immense artistic activity. Could this be an expression of a general characteristic of man?" [10]

---

[9] Roger Lewin, *Spuren der Menschwerdung* (*Human Evolution*), German edition p. 144. **Note: This is translated back into English, as the original version of this edition is not present.**
[10] Emmanuel Anati, *Höhlenmalerei* ("Cave paintings"), p. 25 f.; p. 38

"Creating forms means living.

Are children not creators who draw directly from the mystery of their feelings, more than the imitator of Greek forms? Are not the savages artists, with their own form, strong as the form of thunder? [...]

The delights and sorrows of man, of peoples are behind the inscriptions, the images, the temples, the cathedrals and masks, behind the musical works, theater plays, and dances. Wherever these are not present, where forms are made empty and groundless, there is no art."

August Macke [11]

[11] in: Klaus Lankheit, Documentary new edition of: *W. Kandinsky & F. Marc: Der Blaue Reiter*, p. 55; 59

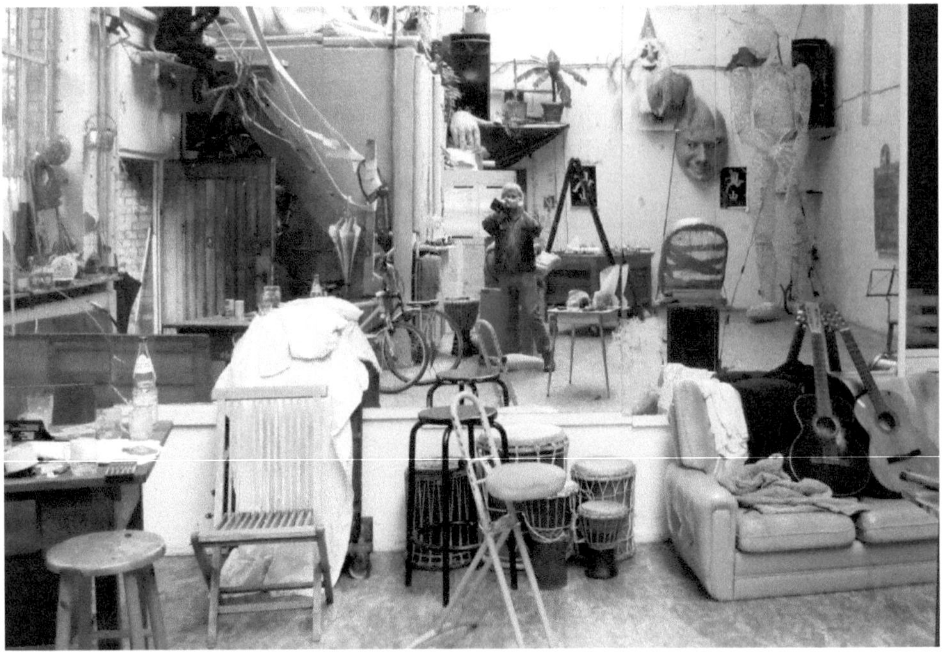

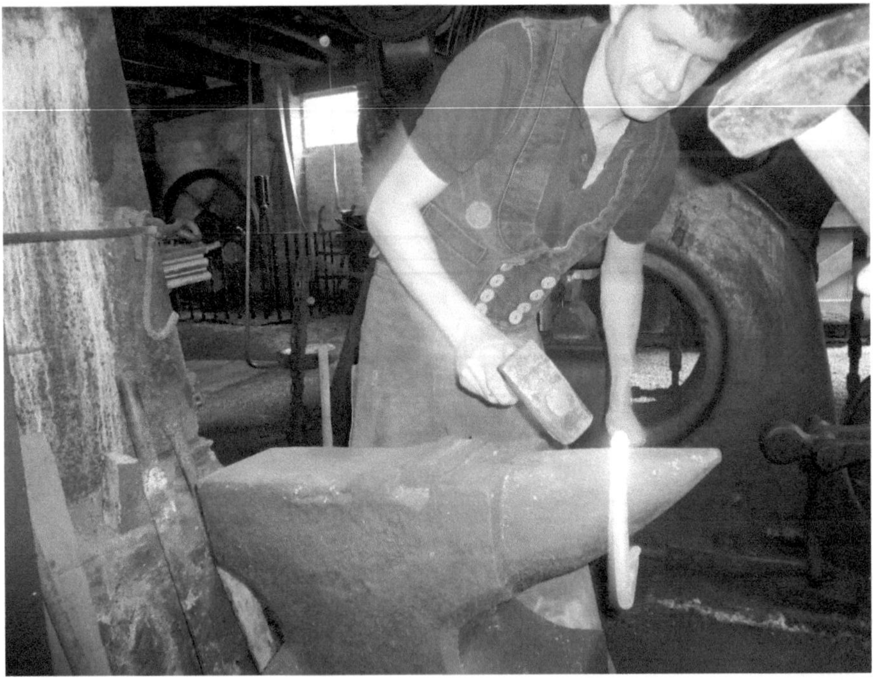

"This spiritually new type of music is about learning from all musical traditions, to detect forgotten backgrounds and to bring to light again the original function of music, its connection to the deepest of human experiences without falling for some naive eclecticism. At present, there is an urge to free the buried primal sources of music which alone can point the way to a new musical experience that encompasses man in his entirety." [12]

"I sensed this sacred or spiritual element even in the movements themselves, the ecstatic trembling, circles, the snake coils and in that sacred shiver that always gripped me when dancing. [...] Belly dance is a spiritual discipline like yoga and tai-chi; it unites women's body, soul and spirit, creating a feminine force field in which healing processes of reintegration may be performed." [13]

---

[12] Peter Michael Hamel, *Durch Musik zum Selbst* ("Discovering the Self through Music"), p. 9
[13] Eluan Ghazal, *Der heilige Tanz* ("Sacred Dance"), p. 9 f.

Theater performing (me, right, about 1994)

"Most importantly, reason must emerge from feeling. You have to return reason to your body. Reason reproducing itself creates a closed cycle that you have to break up through feedback with feeling." [14]

"Dancing: Language of the soul through the body, language of the spirit through the body, expression of the indescribable - art." [15]

---

[14] Min Tanaka, in: Michael Haerdter & Sumie Kawai, *Butoh*, p. 79
[15] Valeria Kratina, in: Ilse Loesch, *Mit Leib und Seele* ("Body and Soul"), p. 197

Extensive global bicycle tours are hugely popular in Telotopia.

"Perhaps the course for my passion for traveling has already been set in my earliest childhood [...].
The discovery of the last wild pieces of land in Europe and outdoor life allowed me to sense during my first walks how much experiencing the wide, open space and the beauty of nature was a mirror image of the inner peace, delight and freedom that I had longed for. For many years, traveling off the beaten tracks was to be one of the few privileges with my internal search. [...]
But most of all, I was intrigued by nomad life. I had the feeling that these people still had the key to those unfathomable expanses. [...]
What's the effort if aching muscles of the first couple of days is followed by the well-being of the forgotten but now reshaped, living body sets in, ready for researching, encountering, all senses honed." [16]

---

[16] Daniel Popp & Jean-Luc Manaud, *Die Wüste lebt* ("The Desert is Alive"), p. 10 - 12

"Traveling means learning how to live" Tuareg proverb [17]

"I also wanted to be a good climber. Out of ambition, drive to move, adventure spirit. [...] I did not go there just for climbing, I had to be on the road. I had to walk freely, hike freely, and be able to climb a mountain every now and then in order to avoid becoming permanently mad in the city."

Reinhold **Messner,** *Dolomiten* ("Dolomites"), p. 114

---

[17] cited in: Désirée v. Trotha, *Heisse Sonne Kalter Mond* ("Hot Sun Cold Moon"), p. 151

"I went to the woods because I wished to live deliberately, to front only the essential facts of life, and see if I could not learn what it had to teach, and not, when I came to die, discover that I had not lived. I did not wish to live what was not life, living is so dear [...]."

Henry D. Thoreau: Walden,
p. 343

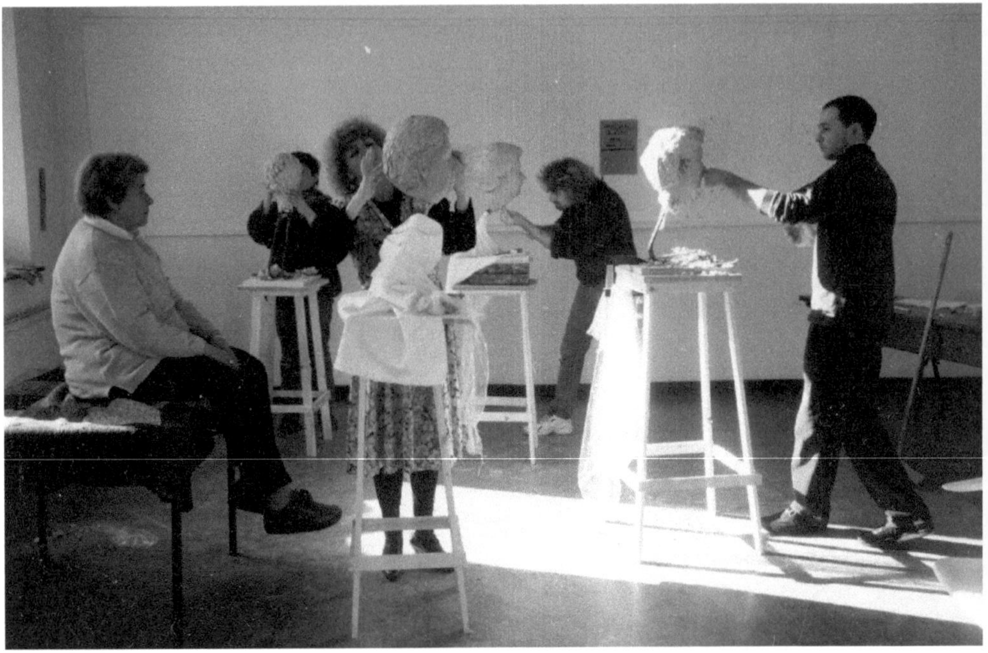

Portrait of the old lady
(above)
cement cast

3.5 Old age

"I learned this, at least, by my experiment; that if one advances confidently in the direction of his dreams, and endeavors to live the life which he has imagined, he will meet with a success unexpected in common hours."

Henry D. Thoreau: Walden, p. 562

The complex of Telotopia is not least of paramount importance to old age. Because it means that old age will, in physical, mental and social terms, not be the price for one's life, but its harvest.

What "old age" means is not formally defined in Telotopia. The figure of 68 in the population structure table merely serves as a guide to the theory. In Telotopia, there is no "old-age pension" in our sense of the word, but *always* provision; therefore, the question of the time of "retirement age" is superfluous.

If you set the age of producing children in Telotopia at 25, you would become grandparents at 50 and great-grandparents at 75. At any rate, there would be a long time available to spend with your grandchildren. If you set the age of producing children at 20, you would become great-grandparents already at 60, giving you a good, active period with your great-grandchildren.

I.
Thus, although physical energy is in decline in old age, but instead you would, under these prerequisites, gain an increasing height of experience at old age until the time of effective senility or death. This decline in energy does not begin just when entering "retirement" but already after the biological thrust to adulthood, perhaps already noticeable in your late twenties, but certainly in your forties. And just as stages emerge in a certain manner here, so in reverse certain stages in levels of achieved experience emerge.

It may well be the case here that with old age emerges a natural tendency for evaluating your "being": a life implying more quiet, and an increasing concentration of the insights considered to be important. This is the reason for a quantitatively reduced but qualitatively developed activity.

In this respect, old age in Telotopia gets, particularly in the educational and social sector, a valued meaning, e.g., in the university sector, in social administration and in all the forms of meditation, supervisions, and consultancies such as also in the medical sector.

---

* My grandmother: her story is told (but in German) by her daughter, Christel Rücker: February 4. A war widow with six children tells her story and her life during the war and the aftermath of the war. A novel. (2018)

The area of assisted living between the Institute for Health (4) and the facility of the Biological Institute (5), see p. 53

see p. 53

II.

I assume that, given the lifestyle of Telotopia, the average lifespan is higher than in our society. But I also assume that the state of health is considerably better. In this respect I fail to see the need for accommodating the possibility of a higher lifespan as a special issue. Given the Telotopian principle of two children per woman/couple, there would be no change in population development in the long run and under these prerequisites there would be no altered provision situation or imbalance in age distribution.

145

Overall, development of old age in Telotopia is rather a fluid process. In Telotopia, people will continue to pursue their activities even at our retirement age, very much according to their needs and their possibilities as well as according to social needs, as previously.

In Telotopia, the special cut in old age, marked as "retirement" in our society, is best linked to the step towards a new life in a housing association when you have given up that type of living. Here, in particular, multi-generational housing associations (e.g., on a farm), a housing association with friends and acquaintances, as well as a housing association in a facility of the Medical Institute are possible.

As everything else, this step is autonomous. But there is the insight that the later you make this change the less you can adapt to it and you would then pay dearly in emotional terms for a too long prolongation of this attitude towards your old-age situation.

Old age in Telotopia is nothing negative, not the price for a wrong way of living. Even if you are confronted with the physical problems of aging in Telotopia, you will be capable of really making use of the development of that experiential dimension.

4 The Entire Complex of Telotopia

4.1   The Boros and their worldwide network organization

Telotopia will, in its actuality, only become permanently possible through worldwide network organization of its Boros. The actual reason for this is in the politico-social sector. More often than not, natural conditions do not regionally provide the necessary resources and are volatile even without distinct upheavals so that a social organization could permanently secure survival at a purely regional level. Ice Age cultures already were therefore linked to larger migrations and networks, as finds have proved. With the food production necessary for sedentism, surpluses could be generated in good times which could then be used for trading. But with the expansion of sedentism and other ownerships, in bad times, problems necessarily occurred because one's survival could only be secured through theft, robbing and violence (therefore, "March" after the Latin warrior god Mars, stocks at that time were frequently depleted after winter, so warring raids remained the only alternative to your *own* starvation).

For this reason, nation states, such as Egypt, for example, historically emerged with the Bronze Age some 5,000 years ago. It was only with the size of these realms that regional supply problems could be balanced to some extent and in those days only these realms attained the temporary power of "conquering", if necessary, other necessary resources (e.g., in those days, bronze) unless they could be maintained through trading. Both this "power" and the dependency on resources (not just for energy) has tremendously increased since industrialization – and therefore also the problem of dictatorships, violence and war. It actually takes a lot to ignore all this in view of constant evidence.

The reason for the global network organization of Telotopia, therefore, actually lies not in the technological-material sector but in that this is eventually the only form of making dictatorships and wars unnecessary, because emerging resource problems can be solved by means other than violence. This not only obtains for crop failures in regions that can be compensated with supplies from other regions and other simple natural disasters such as storm damage, flooding, etc. This obtains, most of all, for such (even quite rare) natural disasters as (super) volcano eruptions or larger meteorite impacts that make resettlements on a larger scale necessary. These problems cannot be solved at regional level, possibly not even at national level. Only a global network federation can be considered as the humanly feasible solution to political, economic and ideological problems.

Such large problems are, of course, rare. In general, no parliament and no panels at world level would be needed. Where Telotopia has been established, these institutions are of no more significance beyond these rare super-disasters. In fact, they serve a supervision to check from this top vantage point what in the structures of global conditions is still unsatisfactory, and how it could perhaps be improved. With this in mind, innovative developments are pursued here, with debates regarding their possible utility for the socio-cultural conditions of Telotopia. In their function of supervision, in Telotopia, the corresponding panels at global level serve rather as coordination and distribution places where requests and suggestions from the lower levels are sifted and, in specifically processed forms, disseminated to the corresponding institutions of the lower levels. An effective decision-making body would be such a parliament at global level, almost singularly in cases of super-disasters where global levels are socially affected.

Overall, that parliament at global level is simply the top level of the overarching organizational structure built by the Boros from below which can really secure the Boros and their cultural level. Completely autarkic and politically "sovereign" small societies such as previous tribes and antique polis city states might in our territories today not be sufficient in parts for survival and may sooner or later lead to permanent small-scale warfare, similar to those recent ones in Papua New Guinea, only at a "higher" level.

Needs of a small-scale autarky, such as a convent facility with self-sufficiency, can well be accommodated at Boro level. Under ordinary general Telotopian conditions it would be no problem if a fellowship wants to withdraw from "secular life" at Boro level. This would also be autonomy and would be possible as part of the popular Telotopian constitution and the respective Boro's regulations.

All in all, this is not about a "back to nature" attitude as people formerly thought in view of historically misguided developments, but a "back to culture" attitude, such as particularly to controlling one's social conditions in collaborative communication. Because this was the decisive factor of human evolutionary development which succeeded in preventing extinction of the hominid form.

Sadly, the gigantic natural disasters at the end of the Ice Age were mainly followed by a substantial loss of culture. Authoritarian structures, dictatorships, violence and power were soon the consequences. Although there also was historical progress in solving the emergency problems that ensued which should not be valued lowly at all, but the actual problem stemming from the loss of culture has so far not been rectified. This will only be the case when the basis of human evolutionary fitness in survival can be reconstructed: the creation of social conditions based on collaborative communication.

This is seen here in the complex of the Boros, but in connection with the superordinate and generally global network organization. On this basis, Telotopia is also capable of space research and travel – but this, here and today, is not really the most urgent issue.

4.2 The common law anchoring of the organization of Telotopia

That a good and simple life can be generally led in Telotopia is based not just in the Boro structure that essentially enables an autonomous life as a person in concrete manageable communities. No less important is that structures have been attained that essentially work permanently. From here, the creation of Telotopia is also essentially based on common law. Until substantial changes become necessary or are desirable, each person and institution can act and do in an autonomous manner as part of the common law structure. From this derives a minor effort in comprehensive organization, which in turn enables actual controllability of the overall structure.

In this sense, it seems to be of major importance that the structures of Telotopia are not subject to constant essential upheavals enforcing everything to constantly restructuring without a visible perspective. In our world today, society has become a huge construction site without any real plan and without any real goal. This reflects the fact that the historical dynamic, due to unresolved conflicts and emergent power struggles, is determined by a flight "forward" or "to the top" ("advanced civilization"), that is, to the helm of *power*. The problem of this paralytic development can only be resolved when, while analyzing history, one arrives at clear notions of meaningful social conditions which will then be built. This cultural-architectural sketch is now about further thinking through the functioning of such a new societal facility.

At any rate, the important issue for functionality of Telotopia seems to be that a workable structure has been established that is essentially integrated into the common lifestyle. For example, we can say that the very ordinary organization of everyday life itself is the most essential element of Telotopian democracy.

Telotopian democracy has its sustainable force, effect and energy in the general self-organization of life. This not only affects the personal and not just the Boro level. It is founded in acquiring again life in general, using suitable structures. In this respect, there is not so much need for determining social processes "from above", which, because everything is involved in global market processes, make everything so tedious in the permanent social reconstruction. Of course, there is in Telotopia still the necessity of its political determination, from the individual Boro through to the highest bodies. But the actual arena of real political provisions due to the established regulations in all bodies is minor that these provisions have become manageable: socially manageable and therefore truly democratic again.

In a certain way, it could be formulated as follows: that nearly all life in Telotopia is designed according to common law. Through the concept oriented towards man a basis emerges where, even beyond the Ice Age small group, the structures of Telotopia are cultural again right up to the highest of bodies. This, of course, presupposes that these structures at the substantial level be not subjected to faster constant restructuring, but again have become the sturdy frame of a vibrant existence. For this reason, further increase in population in Telotopia is generally precluded, from which in principle the limit is two children per woman.

These "structures" are, however, not about "stone", as was endeavored in the Mesolithic (megalith culture: from which the concept of the "state" [= "steh^{e}n" - "stone"] is derived), in order to master the chaos problems arising from the previous natural upheavals at the end of the Ice Age. People did not have the experience of processing those upheavals in a different manner than through the attempt to enshrine the conditions. This concept has worked in the long run in Australia only. In the Middle East, this approach has, however, become the very cause of – now self-inflicted – social chaos problems in view of the constantly ongoing natural changes.

In view of this, we can say, given today's overview of human evolution and history, that only anchoring the structures in anthropologically based social conditions and general democratic self-regulation is qualified for offering more than just short-term social stability as do authoritarian and dictatorial governments at best. 100 years and a few centuries may be quite a long time from a personal viewpoint, but in evolutionary terms it is just an instant. Neanderthal man already had working social conditions over tens of thousands of years. These periods of time are, biologically, the minimum of the order of magnitude before one can speak of a working culture and, unlike the Old Cultures, no alleged "advanced civilization" has provided this working evidence. This seems to be precluded because it has always been built "from the top". But I'm convinced that, given a working basis, as I can see it in the Boro complex, an actual advanced civilization is permanently possible. However, this presupposed an established common law practice – and this is rooted in vividness and capable social and relationship conditions.

The common law complex of Telotopia means that there is a specific framework on all levels which has established itself as common practice and obtains as a reference to present behavior and immediate decisions. Within that framework, then, all people and bodies can act according to their insights and needs, as long as this does not infringe upon the Constitution (human dignity, ecology) or upon concrete provisions (see below).

This general principle makes the entire Telotopian social life simple and vivid. Each adult person and institution knows essentially from common experience what the regulations look like; and from this they can fashion their lives within that framework in an autonomous manner. Therefore, it doesn't take huge administration bureaucracy. This general principle also includes the ecologic sector here. At the basic level of Telotopia, money is not needed, not really even for traveling (see more under → 4.3.4). Life here is for the better part simple and patent. The problems of social neglect such as violence, poverty, social misery, etc. do not exist. Even higher material interests can be redeemed if interested, but this affects more specific regulations (see below).

This common law complex of Telotopia furthermore breaks into specific "categories", basically as follows:

Category 1: In this category, no general problems are familiar or visible. Enough food, products, etc. are available here. Within this framework, people can act in an autonomous manner.

Category 2: In this category, there are no problems within the usual range but, depending on weather conditions in the annual cycle, limits may be reached. With certain tendencies, these developments should be kept an eye on. If necessary, a higher category (3 ff.) may need to be applied.

Category 3: In this category, an eye should be generally kept on the respective processes. Here, the plans are generally possible or the products are generally available. But agreements and, if necessary, planning or even resolutions in the respectively responsible panels are required for this. This would obtain for creating a small settlement in a different location, or for special materials for construction which have to be supplied from outside. This also obtains for personal orders for special products (e.g., on the Internet). Here, purchase may be linked to special terms which in our society equal a "price", for example, which in Telotopia is organized in a different manner, however.).

Category 4: The processes or products of this category are not within the common law level. Generally, they are well possible, but linked to a process of decision-making. In this case, an application would have to be made to the Boro parliament or by a Boro to the regional parliament, etc.

Category 5 includes realities that are linked to even more extensive analyses, debates, consultations and parliamentary decisions. This would obtain, for example, for the question of building a new civic hall, a a railway line, etc.; i.e., projects associated with extra-ordinary expenditure and that need to be solved accordingly.

Category 6 is linked to emergency issues, e.g., special natural disasters. Here, the corresponding specific decisions and measures become necessary.

Above all, Category 6 makes it visible that the categories on the different organizational levels of Telotopia can vary quite a lot. A Category 6, positioned for district level, could be classified as Category 4 or 5 at county level (for these decision levels, see → 4.4.3).

So, categorization plays a role both regarding urgency and regarding the scope of organizational processes. Accordingly, that categorization might actually be positioned in an even more complex manner in practice. Yet this makes this system simple, because most things fall within Categories 1-3 and even Category 4 is on the level of *common* institutional work of parliaments or expert panels. Category 5 processes are relatively rare, but the institutions are basically prepared for this as well.

4.3.3 The political level: Administration and decision-making structures

4.3.3.1 Basics

At the beginning of this section I want to make clear that "democracy" here actually refers to controlling one's social conditions on the basis of "collaborative communication".

The development of controlling one's conditions based on collaborative communication was the crucial moment of human evolutionary development in severing from genetic behavior control at animal level. Obviously, it was the *only biological* alternative to controlling one's social life based on power, social hierarchies, competitive struggles, and violence. For it was with the latter that the stage of hominids (after apes) preceding human evolution, via its very new technological intelligence met, over time, its evolutionary end after some temporary success. Due to the neurological contexts in the behavior system, a corresponding problem also inevitably occurred with our species, Homo sapiens, where collaborative, actual communication is not mastered. [18]

Given the ruinously emergent social conditions, severance from genetic behavior control which established human evolutionary development occurred about 0.5 million years ago. But only empowerment to collaborative communication attained the crucial evolutionary solution. Only this was qualified, with this higher cerebrum system, to generate productive social life.

---

[18] I am speaking here of "actual" communication because mere "talking" is by far and away anything but communication. This becomes visible not just with regards to foreign languages.

Due to a very specific linguistic development, this empowerment as the central content of "culture" was finally reached shortly before our species, Homo sapiens, appeared: with its *cultural* disposition, our species, Homo sapiens, was the evolutionary product of this empowerment.

Therefore, regarding social control, it is **indispensable** to anchor the social basis essentially in a life form that can be organized in an autonomous manner, being manageable in collaborative communication. The Boros, their subdivision and their coordination in the closer environment serve this purpose. Here "democracy", however, **essentially** does **not** imply a **policy** that "governs" the population's lifestyle from above, based on occasional "elections", which still continues the feudal form. In fact, in Telotopia, it implies a structure that essentially enables communal communicated self-organization. In this form, the crucial human evolutionary development remains secured as the basis, which alone can guarantee permanent and productive social conditions.

However, this cannot completely replace the principle of delegation that emerged at the beginning of historical evolution. The genesis of historic progress goes back to the principle of delegation. Not only was this principle of delegation necessary at the end of the Ice Age in order to avoid fights with the surrounding social associations by arrangement when resources became scarce. Even more significant for historical evolution was the positive aspect that, based on the principle of delegation, completely new opportunities in organizing resources emerged. Not only did this solve the resource problems that emerged, it was also the reason for historical progress. The immense megalith complex of Göbekli Tepe (Turkey/Syria border), whose construction began around 9,6000 B.C. and which was already larger than the considerably later built Stonehenge, is an example of this. Various materials, but even more so the linguistic contexts between the later language families prove the tremendous reach of the Göbekli Tepe network organization. For more than one and a half millennia, the Göbekli Tepe network succeeded in bringing peace and progress to the Near East and, with its social and practical techniques like cultivating wheat, it created the cultural foundations of civilizational evolution.

Through its evolution, Göbekli Tepe proves, however, also the shift of the principle of delegation to the emergence of power and domination. This problem arises by necessity, as it were, when more is to be mastered in organizational terms than can be commonly communicated. One can experience this today already in the smallest of communities and associations.

In its expanse and the quantity of involved associations and the necessary clarifications, coordination work at Göbekli Tepe became too complex with increasing population and the advent of food production, and all this could no longer be understood and decided on the population base. The Göbekli Tepe parliament got more and more out of control, becoming a largely autonomous "government". But this was the beginning of the downfall of Göbekli Tepe at about 8,800 B.C. Many units that due to their distance no longer were immediately affected by this coordination (as probably the later Sumerians) were ruled out from direct participation. This is proven through the considerably lower construction activities in Göbekli Tepe which end completely at around 8,000 B.C. Details can be gleaned from the historical linguistic development. [19]

4.3.3.2 On Telboro and Telotopia

In Telotopia, the danger of the principle of delegation getting out of control might be overcome in that it has a largely structured form of self-organization at the basic level. Even if the principle of delegation there has extremely important functions, the scale of its decision-making relations remains manageable. This manageability is the crucial moment here. Through it the danger of the principle of delegation turning into rule from above has been averted.

Once this problem has been solved, the network organization has the advantage, as in historical evolution, to avoid fights about resources

---

[19] For this, see my book on "Mebuntu"

and social control and to produce technological and cultural developments that become possible only by an inter-regional organization.

Such an inter-regional organization is indispensable for an indeterminate time also with the population size and density arising by now under such realities. It's not realistic that the Boros could offer quality of life without an extensive organization and would be capable of existing at all in the long run. This inter-regional organization (including law, economy and production) can, however, not be democratically controlled without the principle of delegation.

At Boro level

At Boro level, the election and delegation system that is common in our society does not play any significant role. In Telotopia, there are no political parties. There is a principle of delegation, though, but this builds upon collaborative communication at common law level, and not upon "general elections". In Telboro, the settlements, the parts of town or village, and the various institutions for specifically corresponding regulations determine their representatives as brokers of the different communication processes.

In the Boro, the (in this case, four) parts of Telboro are the crucial intermediate structure. The representatives of the settlements and institutions in the respective part of town determine their representative in the Boro council at their meetings. The type of election, that of representation, the number of their representatives and their tasks can vary considerably, depending on realities. For decisions that generally affect the Boro special general assemblies will be held at local level. Where the consensus principle is not working and decisions have to be immediately made, those present will choose a specific number of representatives, depending on tasks, who will represent the position of the inhabitants of that part of town at Boro level and who will brief the inhabitants of the discussions at Boro level.

The Boro council consists of these representatives of all parts of town and, if necessary, with specific factual issues, even of representatives of the corresponding expert institute.

These representatives perform a bridge function here to communicate the communication process between individuals and the Boro level in both directions. Where possible, a consensus is found with those decisions. Should an immediately necessary decision not find any consensus, a majority decision may, in case of emergency, reverted to. However, this refers only to individual factual questions or extraordinary situations (e.g., special natural events).

The delegation system

The actual delegation system will only become truly significant in the organizational structures above the Boros. This commences at municipal level, formed from multiple Boros, and continues up to district level as coordinating multiple municipal associations. The municipal and district levels are common part of Boro everyday business, with a lot of information passing through this. Yet these levels are not integrated that closely into everyday life. For example, proven people taking responsibility here, pursuing the control processes of these levels and communicating the decisions becomes relevant. This, of course, holds true all the more at the higher levels of coordination.

This principle of delegation is not, however, via a political party system and is not based on general elections, but through the principle of mandates. The **council** and the extended **forum** of the municipal level, formed from multiple Boros, consist of representatives (delegates) of the connected Boros. Basically, then, the respective Boro council will elect its representatives at the municipal level. But the option to de-elect these representatives at the general Boro level is available in case doubts arise as to whether an individual is sufficiently trustworthy and/or knows how to include the position to be represented in the panels. A sufficient trust relationship is absolutely crucial for the principle of delegation; even more so, the higher the level of the organizational structure.

But more specifically, it is actually the Boro council (including its representative from the parts of town) that is best familiar with the work of the Boro representative in the municipal association. An image campaign for an election cannot catch on politically anywhere there.

160

The delegated people are actually known here, and also predictable. The Boro council is most likely to have the expertise of predicting the skills of its representatives; therefore, in principle, it will envoy the most seasoned and proven Boro representatives to the municipal and district councils.

This is not about the individual himself, but about the fact that a Boro is represented in the control processes of a municipal association. This means that this representation can be constantly alternating, or even that the Boro council sends the respectively technically most qualified individual for specific decision-making in the municipal council.

Generally, however, it is common for a representative to attend the municipal council for a time, because in this manner the best insight into the workings of the municipal council and therefore an expertise in this field can be achieved. But the municipal council, like the Boro council, only deals with the common control processes. Special decisions are discussed and, if necessary, taken rather at forum level with a higher number of representatives. For particularly far-reaching and momentous decisions (e.g., at particular expenditure), specific committees (as in our society) will be set up which are to highlight the decisive aspects. In such contexts, even elections or referendums which determine the decision can be held at Boro level.

So, this is not a rigid system regarding the control of its conditions. In fact, depending on decisions to be made, an attempt will be made to put the principle of "collaborative communication" in the most suitable form into practice. The common law categorization comes in helpful here. For this ensures that people do not get bogged down in trivial or even completely unimportant details, but that the truly relevant decision-making processes are understood and discussed in order to reach a (tending towards) consensus for a decision where possible.

In Telotopia, the essence of the control processes takes place at the lowest levels: perhaps 60% at Boro level, 20% at municipal level, 9% at district level, and 4% at district level (today's governmental districts). In this way, most of ordinary life at population level (of the Boros) remains directly visible in that important decisions at district and county level are made public via the representative at Boro level, and are genuinely accessible or manageable. The emergence of a power complex would be evident in corresponding buildings and "security facilities", for example, and would not be completely covered up and remain unknown. Since Telotopian life works in this manner at a global level, the population can remain the actual democratic "sovereign".

The organizational structures above county level, through to the global forum, play a qualitatively significant role, but little in terms of quantity. In this way, they remain manageable and therefore controllable from below.

Generally, on the one hand, these structures are only for coordination of the respective associations below them. On the other hand, they also serve as politico-economic control of firms active in production and specific activities at the corresponding level, e.g., in ore smelting and steel production at state level, production of specific parts in computing, possibly at global level, etc. The firms are internally independent institutions, but their financing and sales orders are via the respectively assigned association (see economy). In this way, they can be democratically controlled, and economically and ecologically ruinous processes can be avoided.

Railroads shall remain of significance in Telotopia.

4.3.4 Production, work, and economy

Basically, life in Telotopia is a form of self-organization. This also includes the economic sector, and Telotopia's constitution and cultural structure are also of fundamental consequences and provisions for its economy and production.

A good degree of DIY of a Boro seems to be the only plausible alternative to an unmanageable system of politics and business. That a humanly unmanageable system of business and politics would not evoke egoistical behavior in developments of power and exploitation, given all noble intentions, would at this juncture be an extremely "idealistic" view that is not covered by historical evolution. Although man is an extremely social being, this basically presupposes concrete social connections with concrete humans. When these foundations are in place, then there is also a willingness to work where there is poverty and injustice.

But it would be negligent to expect that people in an unmanageable system would be willing in the long run to accept trouble and disadvantages if they can personally avoid these. Under unmanageable conditions, the concrete reference of social feeling is lost and once people have realized that advantages can be obtained elsewhere, a socio-dynamic in the struggle for one's own advantages can hardly be avoided and stopped. This problem emerged, with global historical impact, as early as 11,000 B.C. in the expansive Middle Mesolithic network of the tribe-rights association at Göbekli Tepe. This was repeated in a new form in the priesthood that followed as the solution approach of the Neolithic Revolution, as well as routinely following all revolutions as far as as these had to cope with unmanageable conditions. The original social motivation that could reach up to one's own sacrifice may not be that long-lasting in unmanageable conditions.

Human social behavior relates to conditions that are linked to concrete communication, reaching as far as real communication processes. This may perfectly go beyond a Boro, but only in combination with manageable organizational structures. Accordingly, the solution of the economic problem is that the essential part of its supply and production sector at one's own Boro level comes with some connections to its neighboring Boros.

In reality, we are not short of production and service offerings at all. As early as the 1830s, during the early stage of industrialization, it was recognized that the economic problem in reality results from a surplus of products and services. But the surplus does not solve any of the "economic" problems just because of this; it actually produces them, from the personal situation through to the state coffers. That enough products and service offers are available does not mean that they are affordable. Thus, starving in front of mountains of unsold food is possible, as are fights and wars through to mutual ruin. The background to this problem is nothing new, however; it is linked right from the start to the logic of historical evolution from the end of the Ice Age, way before any "capitalism".

Insofar as one is interested in a solution of the economic problems – and the ecological problems resulting from this, as early as 8,000 years ago – one has to leave the unconscious reflex of striving to solve these through increased surplus of production and work and, today, even monetarization. This problem becomes solvable only when one eventually realizes that the original emergency problems result from the gigantic natural disasters at the end of the Ice Age which, sadly, lasted at least for two millennia so that the emergency in consciousness, language and behavior became "culture". From the foundations, the emergency of the entire historical evolution continues to this day, even though the natural disasters at the end of the Ice Age have long gone. The surplus, however, proves that the entire economic problems which led right up to fascism and the two world wars are completely unnecessary and today are merely the *social* product of one's own stupidity (i.e., the *socially* "self-inflicted immaturity") (individuals can really not withdraw from that). In former times, people could not know better. But now we have an overview *per se* of historical evolution going far beyond the evolution of man and even of primates, which might be utilized.

Regarding the economy and production, Telotopia means, depending on needs, that about 90 - 95% of our present work and production become obsolete. First of all, we should mention armaments production as well as over 99% of "security services" (the military, etc.) here, of transportation and in the province of administration and sales. In Telboro, everything can be reached on foot. Even the use of bicycles for such purposes is rare. Those bicycles that can be borrowed from the Boro are more used for performing duties in other Boros or for trips and tours. Since life here is no longer determined from above and people have again become capable of joint self-organization, the essential part of "administration" is simply part of a concrete way of life.

As is visible to experts, in reality there is rather the problem of what *meaningful* activities can be pursued with all that available time without all those artificial business operations intended to counter business collapse. Given common socialization, education and schooling, this is indeed a serious problem.

In view of the actual realities, however, the economic, production and work sector must be conceived entirely differently with regards to Telotopia. There is no longer just a richly endowed emergency culture. Life there is simple in many respects, just as real life itself is. But it is a "rich" life regarding the very actual thing: rich in social, cultural and relationship quality – just as in the result of human evolutionary development with the actual sense of "culture", only extended with the positive moments of historical development towards an actual advanced civilization.

Telotopia is not ruled by an anti-technology attitude. In Telotopia, the entire previous historical technology, research and industrialization are accepted and continued as far as as this seems to be actually meaningful, e.g., when using computers and the Internet. However, what really appears to be advantageous and desirable in technology and industrial production (even in the food production sector) must be demonstrated in a completely new form, that is, when on the one hand prices are no longer determined by social and economic exploitation and, on the other hand, wages and revenues are no longer determined by participation in that exploitation.

No doubt this has also some unpleasant aspects. Although Telotopia will not have to fully relinquish bananas from America in our territory, but these will become again luxury items.

In Telotopia, the surplus potential in production and services will not be used to increase economic problems, i.e., power relations. Because, given a suitable organizational creation, at this level there are no survival issues regarding food and work that go beyond the corresponding historical misguided developments, the techno-material potential that has already emerged is used in Telotopia for capable social life which corresponds to the genuinely authentic needs of man and the respectively concrete men. Basically, at any rate, this initially means creating child-friendly conditions (in the context of children's socialization stage).

Today's drift towards large cities has social, economic as well as cultural reasons; these become essentially obsolete in Telotopia. However, in Telotopia, there are both technological and industrial as well as urban "functional centers" ($\rightarrow$ 4.4.2). In these functional centers, people can pursue "more sophisticated" activities because these are connected to technologically more sophisticated equipment (e.g., in medical institutions) and productions.

In the form of "functional centers", the needs of more demanding tasks and activities that go beyond the usual Boros can be met, as more advanced functions and productions are also possible there.

Basically, we can only say here that in Telotopia all this is possible in cultural and technological terms, which even today is possible in terms of desirability, but without the – by now ruinous – dimension of downsides. Even in Telotopia, high-tech, as in space research, will still be performed.

In Telotopia, all that technology (like computer technology) and industrial production (e.g., of metals, engines, etc.) will be utilized. But, given today's economy, it's no longer that easy to resolve whether DIY or industrial production involves greater effort.

However, since production in Telotopia is no longer linked to fighting for power and survival (such as economically and, for example, in armaments technology), people can resolve in collaborative communication what of production appears to be desirable in what form and is, respectively, desired. In the long run, experience will be had here of how to procure these needs under the new realities and which forms of organization, production, work and technology prove to be optimal on the whole.

In Telotopia, the principle exists to create as much as possible at the level of DIY for people and a Boro, and preferably directly on site (e.g., a smaller wind turbine directly at a farm). This, however, is primarily rooted in social life and in the motive of the quality of life.

Complete self-sufficiency of a Boro would be uneconomic and does not seem to be desirable on the whole. A Boro as a single reference space would be too limited in different respects and could not offer any cultural level in the long run. A Boro can only be kept alive based on a more extensive network (see below).

There will definitely be larger forms of production and industry in Telotopia. This would affect, in any case, metal processing and production of engines and computers, but maybe also production of grains, etc. In certain production lines centralization seems to be favorable (e.g., glass, metal processing) and sometimes even absolutely indispensable due to the tremendous expenditure of specific technology (computer parts). This will be created according to the raw material deposits and further processing. In vehicle manufacturing, this would be conceivable in that the metals and specific parts are produced at a supranational level and other specific parts in the larger regional context and that car body construction is regional and the final stage of completion and painting in the Boro workshop (at the "freight depot"), which is involved with certain types of maintenance and repair (even trains, bicycles, etc.)

It can be assumed that certain tasks are desired and enjoyable. This can be the case, for example, when forging, painting, assembling parts into a vehicle, repairing and restoring, as is familiar in the context of vintage cars or in art (e.g., fantasy machines).

Where and as far as this is the case, such work will be assigned to the Boro or its closer environs.

Where there is no relevant interest in such work, but in the product, it will be industrially manufactured. Even with these types of production facilities we will see the level of interest in it. Where work cannot be covered by intrinsic motivation but with a need for products, Telotopia always operates with forms of "remuneration". This may come in the form of a "wage" and/or providing special housing options, luxury items (e.g., special wines or whiskeys or remote import items like bananas).

So, in Telotopia, certain types of work, education/training and activities are an opportunity to obtain special housing options, jobs and/or products.

But all in all, this is linked to a crucially different overall concept. In Telotopia, everything is created as well as possible in such a manner that it corresponds to authentic needs; but the personal will never be able to dominate public circumstances and thus other people beyond one's own private sphere. You cannot win or lose a status in Telotopia.

The better remunerations are not (as under power relations) meant to produce inauthentic conditions by manipulation. Such effects would be immediately countered with the corresponding perceptions. But it is also legitimate in Telotopia to lead a most simple or externally sophisticated lifestyle, as personal autonomy that affects one's own personal life.

Telotopian culture is (therefore) oriented towards fostering and supporting the personal where possible because the human optimum is conceived also with regards to social life. This orientation also affects material equipment and remuneration that make the most varied of lifestyles and needs possible. There is neither envy of simple life nor of living in upper-class conditions, because everything is open to anyone and everyone chooses their own path. In Telotopia, one may spend one's day angling, living in a hut and get simple wine, for example.

Anyone who wants something sophisticated must do something sophisticated to achieve this, depending on the respective scale, all in a natural economy without social disadvantage and preference.

Different needs are legitimate here and also welcome, but only insofar as they relate to one's personal autonomy. Everything that is of effective consequences regarding social life or nature is subject to the social and ecological provisions of Telotopia. Many things are possible here, as part of common law, even absolutely easy and, besides, depending on the respective agreements or, if necessary, on specific decisions of the responsible administration or council meeting.

So, attaining more sophisticated options and products is possible through specific activities. But accumulating properties exceeding direct personal need is never possible in Telotopia. In Telotopia, land, houses, firms with employees – anything affecting public life cannot become private property or heritable. Houses are made available for utilization only through the respective agreements in such a manner that everyone can set up their lives well.

Within a certain smaller framework there are also new architectural projects that can be privately initiated and be made available for private use. However, they will never become property, but these buildings need not be financed privately anyway. Even castles can, if interested, analogously leased for living purposes to descendants within a specific framework, but this is not connected to more privileges. The descendants would hardly be able to adequately maintain the castle with their own work, let alone keep it structurally sound. In this respect, this will possibly be taken as the "cultural heritage" in public form and therefore be publicly made available (e.g., as a museum and for events). In Telotopia, "nobility" is viewed, from a complete distance, as a purely historical phenomenon which has, fortunately, eventually be overcome.

Our private property of land and resources is based, in any case, at least originally on an illegitimate acquisition through power and violence; it is also the hotbed of power and violence. The same is true at territorial state level. In Telotopia, this is considered as contradicting to a democratic order and (therefore) a violation of human rights.

In Telotopia, land and natural resources are mankind's common property (which also includes future generations, from which derives the principle of sustainability). Even a Boro only has the right to its *own social autonomy* as part of the Telotopian constitution. It does not "own" its territory and the possible natural resources in its territory. This is of consequence, for example, if relevant natural upheavals make reorganizing the land (an area) necessary. In this case, depending on the scope of the land to be distributed, a corresponding superordinate organization of Telotopia has been assigned the task of performing, in accord with the affected Boros, a new territorial division or restructuring of the Boros there, or offering people an entirely new territory. Even natural resources are managed, also according to type and scope of use, at a corresponding high organizational level; i.e., very rare natural resources at the topmost levels. Natural reserves are also assigned to a corresponding high body, depending on their size and their specifics.

Basically, the land intended for living is split among the Boros. Here, that land is essentially intended for the population's self-organization. A certain part of production and/or services is used to enable supralocal organization, also as an exchange value for receiving products and services from outside (e.g., seasonal workers, specialists or computers, vehicles).

Here, the "values" are not, however, set as abstract and equal ones for Boros and states, but natural topography is also considered (climate, altitude, soil quality, etc.). The bases of fees and allocations are set in annual administrative budgets. This would not be uncomplicated in itself, but organization in Telotopia has been established in that most things are regulated according to common law, unless larger natural disasters overthrow these regulations.

For the population this means that land per se is available for free, but (in our regions) not infinitely. To some extent, division of land is determined by the Boros and creation of the respective Boro. Overall, the structure is so versatile that something is available to everyone at the more common level. But additionally, it is also possible to select other regions of one's choice for traveling, temporary stays or even permanent residence, depending on availability. These can be regions with large nature reserves or urban complexes, by the sea or in the mountains and different countries with their respective realities and traditions. In general, this is easier than today, at least for temporary stays, since such a temporary change from the age of 35 or 40 is more common in Telotopia because people want to discover, at least temporarily, other regions and conditions. This is frequently also in combination with particular or simply other vocational activities.

In principle, common law regulation applies for all this. In the section of Category 1, this is no problem at all. This obtains for traveling, accommodation in the Boros, temporary stays in other Boros, and also for permanent resettlement.

Generally, the common economy of Telotopia can essentially do without money. The general economic principle of Telotopia consists in exchanging products and services. However, the values are not set in an abstract manner here.

Here the principle of common law categories comes into play. On the simple level and with Category 1, it is common for a person, after childhood, to make contributions according to their possibilities and sensitivities. Helping out or doing something is something that is perceived as purely human and natural. In Telotopia, both parties (supplier and demand) or all parties don't want to exploit anyone. But tourism is also possible. Where people want to contribute no or little service, utilization can be compensated against payment.

Moreover, the respective budgets of the different organizational levels (see below) play a role in Telotopian economy.) As already mentioned, these annual (and seasonally subdivided) budget designs are initially based on the empirical values of the past, which are then modified by intended or even expected changes.

In these budgets, various "allocations" are set. This means, for example, that a Boro provides x tons of potatoes, y tons of apples and z hours of services (e.g., seasonal workers and specialists) to the regional organization and the national organization, and receives flour and sugar from the regional organization and computers and technology from the national organization. All this is, of course, significantly more complex regarding the products and the brokering bodies.

All this would be quite complicated, but it's actually quite simple with established conditions, because each instance has fairly precise foundations for its schedules and work. The common fluctuations with harvests and with fashions have been considered. The great advantage of this system is that production and work can be adjusted extremely accurately to concrete human needs and concrete social requirements in social justice and in compliance with its constitution.

With each budget plan, services and products from **Category 3** and higher are always termed with a type of "price/value" which can be accommodated as evidence for exchange and trade. These prices and values, however, are not abstract, fixed ones. On the one hand, they can be negotiated, underlying also the principle of supply and demand. However, they always refer to a respective budget plan. Also, revenue is initially always valid only within that respective budget plan.

This means that each body, with its budget plan (be that a Boro or state administration) always functions as a bank with its own currency system, as it were. These currency systems have different categorizations which are to do with both availability of products and their type. Exchanging currencies is possible, but this is part of the tasks of the respective administration. In certain respects, processing these transactions is even linked with the main activity of the respective administrations which, however, due to their common law creation is quite feasible.

In this way, the economic aspect is prevented from becoming independent of the social aspect, wherein lies one of the paramount reasons for wars and socially paralyzing processes.

This Telotopian system enables those who want it to receive particularly good housing, residential estates, wines, furniture, ceramics, artworks, etc. and other, especially qualitative or expensive products for private need through appropriate work commitment and/or vocational qualifications. But this may prevent the subject/personal/private area from socially sprawling into power and exploitation over the subject/personal/private area, thereby ruining economic conditions. Speculation with land, houses, resources and vital foodstuffs is not possible in Telotopia, or it would, if necessary, be considered as a question of "offense", "attempted blackmailing", etc. It should not be forgotten that such practices may exceed the consequences of individual murders, and can therefore never be considered to be less problematic.

Special products or services can, within certain limits, also be immediately obtained for special services or products (even artwork). This can also be designed as a "gift economy"; it need not necessarily be linked to offsets.

At this point, something like "money" appears. Here it might be conceivable that in Telotopia a kind of cash-in checks, if necessary, in the form of bank cards as we know them, are used. These were used for payments like specific activities or sales for paying in.

A system that in Telotopia corresponds to the other organizational system is connected to these cards. When you live in a Boro or stay there as a guest, you would create an account with the administration to which the respective Boro bank card refers. When traveling you would use bank cards of a correspondingly high body; but this is not recommended as a general solution due to higher administrative effort and the corresponding higher fees. On arrival in a Boro you would set the credits of this card with the local Boro bank as credits and when leaving you would rebook the balance on site back to the currency of the other card (like changing currencies in our society). Specific businesses and activities can, however, also be transferred via Internet through analogous logic.

In this way, the economic area can be reintegrated into its self-organization (in the budgets of the different organizational stages), preventing the economy from getting out of control.

This regulation sounds complicated, but it's actually less complicated than under our present conditions. This can be seen in that the bulk of activities and products is not subjected to any explicit economy. But special requests can also be fulfilled through this. For this, "explicit economy" is used which represents something like "money". Here, money has become again a medium of exchange, integrated into social life, like the idea behind money, but not its reality. It is to be hoped that we will not have to experience our money not having any value in itself in order to get an idea of this.

4.4   Superordinate organization

4.4.1   The regional complex of the Boros

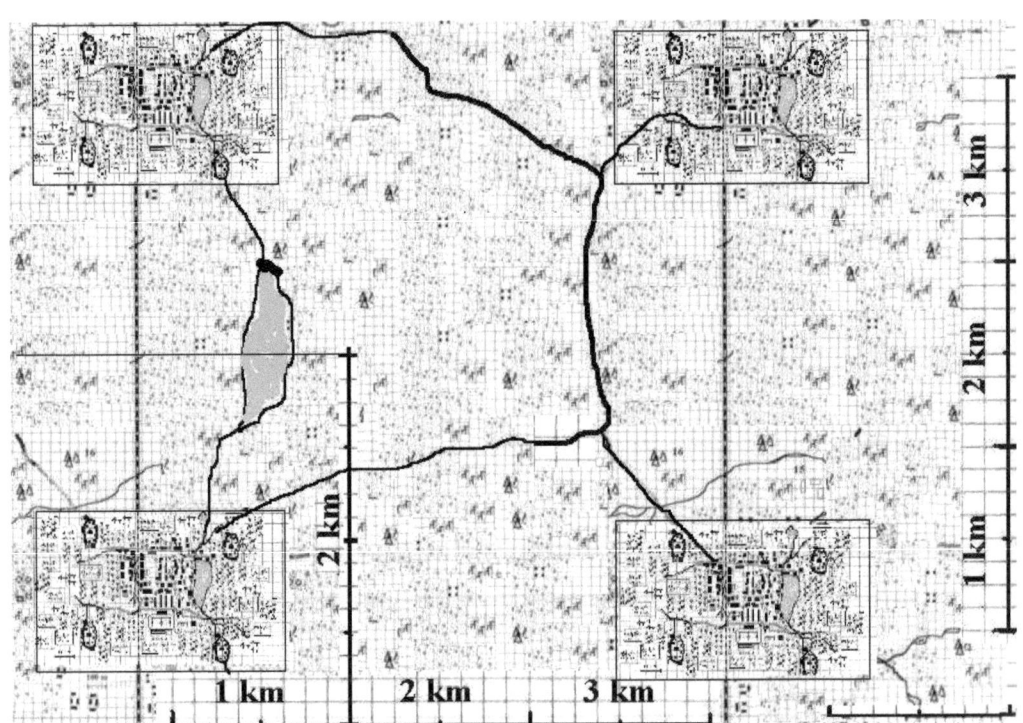

*Scheme of a **territory covering 4 Boros** with a **Boro area of 3km x 3km** (this would have a population density almost twice as high as that of the Federal Republic of Germany, or FRG)*

Boro with 4,000 inhabitants: at 2 km x 2 km =1000 inhabitants/km²
at 3 km x 3 km = 444 inhabitants/km²
at 4 km x 4 km = 250 inhabitants/km²
at 5 km x 5 km = 160 inhabitants/km²

With a population density like the current on in the FRG with about 231 inhabitants/km² (2022: 232 inhabitants/km²), this would make an **average** of

- a Boro area of 4.16 km x 4.16 km = 17.3 km²
- a route of about **4.16 km** from one Boro center
       to the next =
- about 3 km from the Boro center **edge** to the next Boro
       center edge (at this diagonal distance this makes about
       5.9 km as well as about 4.2 km **land** area)

We would thus tend to have, in general, settlement patterns as exist, in our society, in the country, e.g., concerning the areas between places. The crucial difference, however, is that each Boro has a more or less urban center. In Telboro, this has, given all its village character, the size of the pedestrian zone/precinct of a small town, with the exception of those areas that require special expenditure.

But a popular Boro may not be up to special orchestras or dancing theaters of our present large cities from a technical perspective. But since art, theater, music, dancing, etc. in Telotopia are humanly integrated right from the start, both in terms of culture and socialization, a Boro may display a level that in our society is only achieved by occasional pioneers.

For ongoing developments, the technical and urban functional centers have been set up. These urban functional centers are justified here by the fact that, for example, four Boros provide a joint main center. The size of the population remains within a kind of Boro in order to keep the principle of tending towards self-organization. Moreover, when creating a Boro and a region, the realities of nature and the historic legacy play, of course, a part.

4.4.2 Technical and urban functional centers

At this stage of discussions, it's not easy to assess the actual consequences of the existence of genuine culture. Initially, the cultural standard of today's cities can be taken as a starting-point. In Telotopia, virtually each "village", i.e., each Boro, has a university with libraries, a kind of zoo and botanic facilities, museums, galleries, stages (artists, dancers, musicians, theater and circus folks). And this would also be only the distinct, institutionalized expression of general cultural life in a Boro which is already taking place in every child-garden park.

In Telotopia that which should preferably exist in each Boro is differentiated from that which is only possible in special form due to effort and/or rarity. As with our culture, it may well be the case that a special museum (possibly due to a local archeological place of discovery or a former company) or even a very specific medical institution (possibly from developing a practice by a luminary) is housed, with regional or national significance, in a very ordinary Boro. However, in Telotopia, just like in our culture, it's not uncommon that special institutions or interurban significance are housed in regional centers and at traffic junctions.

In Telotopia, there are various forms of "functional centers". One kind of functional center is connected to technology, production or logistics, such as a company, an industrial estate, or a port facility. The other kind, the "urban functional centers", are linked with social and/or cultural functions such as administrations at the higher level (region, state, etc.), university, shopping centers, museums, traffic junctions, etc.

Above: An industrial functional center
Below: A great urban functional center (shopping area)

Urban functional centers

These "urban functional centers" may continue our present large cities; however, in Telotopia they are, in terms of organization, not a "city" in our sense of the word. In Telotopia, these "urban functional centers" are the joint center of multiple Boros which (similar to our neighborhoods) are centered around that center in an eccentric structure.

The difference is in administration. Even if some Boros are similar to our neighborhoods in their continuation of today's city facilities, the actual sovereignty is with the Boros here. The "urban functional centers" are, like the rural areas and the technical functional centers, administered at district, regional or state level, depending on their size or significance, and actually democratically governed by the Boros.

Such an urban functional center might be created in connection with four Boros. This would make, in our sense, a "town size" of 16,000 inhabitants and, with 4,000 further "guests" of the functional center who work, study and, if necessary, even live there in addition for a limited period, 20,000 inhabitants. In an expanded urban functional center, 12 Boros might be connected to it (= 48,000 inhabitants and, possibly, 12,000 guests = 60,000 inhabitants). This is not few, because here only the **immediate** area surrounding the urban functional centers is counted and not the entire "incorporations", that generally produce the high figures of our cities (in Germany).

Of these specific links, it seems to be possible to keep the historically valuable area of our cities in Telotopia, and to continue it in a new and better way. In Telotopia, the other *present* neighborhoods would become centers in their own right to a comparable principle. Of course, there would, around these centers, be the need for thinning out of building and settlements in order to create a Boro structure – which surely, over time, would quite naturally grow from the needs of the population.

The previous run on cities was linked with jobs, functions and earning options there, and for this, people were frequently prepared to accept bad quality of life in the urban neighborhoods. These advantages no longer exist in Telotopia. On the contrary, life in these urban neighborhoods would be quite disadvantageous there, because you would not be able to produce much yourself there and because there would be only little need for the "functions" there, since this would be (better) covered by the actual centers. So, there would be few corresponding revenues or remunerations there. Here, the new Boros can offer significantly more of quality of life and maintenance options.

The effective purpose of the functional centers in Telotopia is that issues are organized here which are needed only sporadically outside of the Boros. This, for instance, affects special production facilities, special organizational centers, special expert institutes with special museums, specialist libraries, and medical institutions. These facilities are organized as joint projects of the Boros of a district or a region and, at an even more specific level, as joint projects of regions and states.

These functional centers can be connected to Boros. But as such, these are clear functional logic such as those of a company, for example. These functional centers are created and maintained by order of the Boros and, accordingly, they are considered part of the Boros' culture. The Boros are and remain the organizational basic structure of Telotopia: *the* humanly feasible and controllable connection between the individual and society. It's the Boros that eventually govern and determine the larger functional centers and also the supra-local organization. Only through this will conditions remain human, democratic and actually mastered, without degenerating as with the historical development of independence and therefore cultural neglect through "power", violence and social hierarchies, the corresponding orchestrations of which in former days were considered to be the epitome of "culture". As much as there are larger (functional) centers in Telotopia which are maintained by the Boros because of specific functions or due to a larger interest among the population, these are still determined by the constitution and legal structure of Telotopia, and will not, as in history, become "power centers" based on exploiting countryside and people.

A larger functional center with a modern means of transportation connecting several Boros, which organize that functional center.

4.4.3 The overall organization of Telotopia at global level

It's only the global constitution of the Boro complex that actually creates general social stability. Only this will prevent terrorist, dictatorial developments, provided there is an effectively democratic foundation. Only this will enable creating the necessary balancing moments in addition to high tech which in natural processes time and again accrue, particularly with natural disasters and climatic upheavals. With such grave processes, it may become necessary to reorganize entire regions. From a mere Boro level and even a mere regional level this would never be possible, which with problems of this nature can lead to nothing other than violent migrations of peoples as in history. For the corresponding reasons, greater territorial system ("states") evolved as early as the Bronze Age.

<u>In Telotopia, the organizational structure is organized as follows:</u>

- the Boro level
- the local level   from multiple Boros
- the district level
- the county level   (e.g., governmental districts)
- the regional level   (e.g., like that of German states)

- the national level   (like medium-sized states)
- the state federation level   (like the USA, India, China, Russia)
   - higher state federation level   as subdivision into Asia
- the continental level   (like Europ. Council; Africa, etc.)
- the global level

This would roughly describe the structural design, connected to specific status forms, which is necessary due to the decision-making structures (see below).

Due to natural conditions, which can also be valid regarding the size of the population, there can be different intermediate levels. Overall, the principle that the higher level is always formed from a **manageable** number of associations of the respective level below it applies. In doing so, this would seldom require more than two dozen. The consequence of this might be that there is an intermediate stage between the Boro and district level. Below that, in areas with very few people, a Boro might at the same time be the district level. This would be of relevance for its representation in the regional parliament. Pure schematism leads us nowhere. Understanding the structures as a means of organizing one's communication and always to create the respectively meaningful and workable structures is part of Telotopian organizational logic.

In Telotopia, generally, this is that a transparent number of Boros forms a "municipal association" for the purpose of supra-local cooperations which in a panel is under the supervision of the representatives of the Boros. Further organizational structure here is similar to that in our culture, the only difference being that the principle of Telotopia builds on the Boros from below. Thus, a transparent number of "districts" forms the "county level". This is under supervision of representatives of the "districts". There may also be a separate controlling panel of representative directly from the Boros. A transparent number of "regions" forms a "state federation" that is under supervision of representatives of the regions, possibly including a controlling panel of representatives of the regions and possibly even of representatives of the Boros. In conflict-ridden combinations, this may also be assigned arbiters from the higher level or even of the neutral kind. This pattern continues upwards.

I assume that this superstructure does not take on any particular dimensions and remains well verifiable from below. This, of course, presupposes that the essential part of the material-organizational culture of Telotopia is at Boro level and district level, and also works based on common law.

Even the county level only has a certain level of coordination with regard to some special tasks, for example, in dealing with larger rivers and in the administration of companies that work at the district level due to their special mechanical equipment. At the even higher levels, this will thin out even further in quantitative terms. If necessary, specific engine production would be at state level and production of particular computer parts such as processors would be at continental or even global level. At the higher level, this is essentially about production sectors which are organized in companies in compliance with the guidelines of democratic decision-making. These companies are working like our companies, only with a democratically determined production scope (unit numbers of vehicles, for instance) in like economic equipment (if necessary, also for research purposes). The political level does not administer these companies. It only determines the framework conditions: the locations, the scope of orders, the budget; it also checks that production is according to desirable manner (e.g., also work conditions, ecological consequences, etc.).

This is also essential based on common law, e.g., with regards to the scope of production. Innovations are quite possible here, but they do not ensue suddenly; instead, they are smoothly integrated into the ongoing process. That their use is slower, then, does not appear to be the problem.

This makes production and its organization with the introduced companies relatively simple and from this arise not too many demands to the political administration of Telotopia. Therefore, the higher levels should also be controllable with a solid democratic foundation like, above all, the presented Boro structure.

Dictionary

This dictionary accommodates individual topics; in this short version, however, only:

On the Telotopian right to children

In a certain manner, we are confronted with human overpopulation, which gives rise to many constraints and ecological problems. This problem of overpopulation can not, as history shows, be solved through violence. A solution can only be conceived in a solidarity-based reception of the difficulties resulting from this.

Also, for reasons of permanence and social stability, further increase in population is precluded for Telotopia. From this follows the principle that the right to children in general is limited to two per woman (children are not compulsory though). This number is already common practice under our conditions.

In individual cases, the exact provision in Telotopia is a thing of the respective territories and realities. Where there is no population growth and pressure, this principle does not require strict provisions. If necessary, the desire to have more children can also be met where people are prepared to live in areas without a higher population. If necessary, such resettlement would also be the outcome where in territories of a strict two-children rule that rule is violated.

This principle of the two-children rule refers to the time until one's own children become parents themselves. Should a child die at a younger age, the right to another child would be legitimate.

Besides, in Telotopia, this principle is not considered to be a purely legal issue. It is well conceivable that the question of a desire for children among adolescents (Stage IV) and young adults (Stage V) is a big issue where the actual statistical child question is solved in that when there is a desire for more than two children, others might accept correspondingly less.

Since, in Telotopia, people in Stage V are living mostly in communes anyway and (beyond personal assets such as photos or home-made ceramics) no inheritances are linked to children, children (as in ancient cultures) are not a topic of birth anyway, but of genuine interpersonal relationships.

A mural: Life
Individual, and free as a tree
And as brothers and sisters like a wood
Is our longing
Nazim Hikmet

"The primeval hope of all history refers to a genuine and therefore absolutely *communal* community of the human race."

Martin Buber, *Der utopische Sozialismus* ("Utopian Socialism"),
p. 241

Literature and notes

Here are just a few notes to info and literature. Overall, a lot of further notes emerge which are, were or could be of significance regarding a New Culture: as part of history, ethnology, human sciences such as psychology and, in the cultural sector, like, among others, H. D. Thoreau, William Morris, Rudolf Steiner, Expressionism, Art Nouveau, Bauhaus, artists like Vincent van Gogh, Paul Gauguin, Friedensreich Hundertwasser, etc. Many things can also be found in biographies. Personally, I find the different approaches and experiments inspiring. You may browse the Internet, libraries and bookshops. This work does not compile an overwhelming bibliography.

On **architecture, see** the Internet

    Tree house hotels
    Tiny house
    Earth mound house

Modern **eco-house** designs (see p. 82, for example):
    solar decathlon europe (Wuppertal) – www.sde21./eu/de

Wikipedia (interesting photos under Commons):

Earth house; specifically: Peter Vetsch (architect)
Earthship (house)
Dwelling cave
Tree house
Tiny house movement
The **Tarot Garden** (Giardino dei Tarocchi, Tuscany)
Hundertwasser (artist, also architecture)

Utopian designs

B.F. **Skinner**, *Walden Two*,
    New York: Hackett Publishing Company 1948
Ernest **Callenbach**, *Ecotopia*, 1975
Aldous **Huxley**, *Island*, London: Chatto & Windus 1962

p.m., *bolo'bolo*, Final edition, Zurich: Verlag Paranoia City,
    1990
P.M. and friends, *Olten - Alles Aussteigen, Ideen für eine Welt*
    ohne Schweiz ("Olten - All align, Ideas for a New World"),
    Zurich: Paranoia City Verlag 1990

Theory and history of utopian projects and experiments

Marie Louise **Berneri**, *Journey Through Utopia*, London:
    Routledge 1950
Ferdinand **Seibt**, *Utopica – Zukunftsvisionen aus der Vergangenheit*
    ("Utopica – Future visions from the past"), Updated new
    edition Munich: Orbis Verlag 2001
Time-Life books: *Visionen und Utopien* ("Visions and Utopias"),
    Cologne: Eco Verlag 1999

Hellmut G. **Haasis**, *Spuren der Besiegten 1* ("Traces of the
    Vanquished 1"), Reinbek: Rowohlt 1984
Christopher **Hill**, *The World Turned Upside Down - Radical Ideas*
    during the English Revolution, London: Maurice Temple
    Smith 1972
Jan **Peters** (Hg.), *Die Geschichte alternativer Projekte von 1800 bis*
    1975 ("The History of Alternativ Projects from 1800 to
    1975"), Berlin 1980
Robert **Landmann,** *Ascona Monte Veritá – Auf der Suche nach*
    dem Paradies ("In Search of Paradise"), Frankfurt/M.,
    Berlin, Wien, 1979
Else **Bramesfeld** et al (ed.), *Gelebte Utopie – Aus dem Leben einer*
    Gemeinschaft: Nach einer Dokumentation von Dore Jacobs
    ("Living Utopia – Notes from the Life of a Community: After
    documentation by Dore Jacobs"), Essen: Klartext Verlag
    1990 - **This was a very interesting historic project!!**

Helen & Scott **Nearing**, *Living the Good Life*, New York:
  Schocken Books 1964
Scott **Nearing**, *The Making of a Radical – A Political
  Autobiography*, New York: Harper and Row 1972

Peter **Maffay,** *Hier und Jetzt: Mein Bild von einer besseren Zukunft*
  ("Here and Now: My Dream of a Better Future"), Cologne
  2020
Henry David **Thoreau,** *Walden, or Life in the Woods*, New York:
  The Viking Press 1947 (reprint)

Günter **Zint** (Hg.), *Republik Freies Wendland* ("The Republic of
  Free Wendland"), Frankfurt/M.: Zweitausendeins 1980

Ulf Erdmann **Ziegler**, *Nackt unter Nackten. Utopien der
  Nacktkultur* ("Nude Among Nudists: Utopias of Nudist
  Culture") *1906 – 1942*, Herrsching, 1992

Martin **Buber**, *Der utopische Sozialismus* ("Utopian Socialism"),
  Cologne 1967

Ernst **Bloch**, *Das Prinzip Hoffnung* ("Principle Hope"), 3 Bände
  (1959), Frankfurt/M.: suhrkamp taschenbuch wissenschaft,
  6th edition 1979   - contains a **"sketch of social utopias"**

Christoph **Besemer**, *Zurück zur Zukunft? Utopische Kommunen,
  Anspruch und Wirklichkeit, Auswertung historischer
  Erfahrungen* ("Back to the Future? Utopian Communes:
  Aspiration and Reality"), Berlin 1981

Rolf **Goetz**, *Von der Landkommune zur Dorfgemeinschaft. Ökolo-
  gische Modelle zwischen Anarchie und Spiritualität* ("From
  Land Commune to Village Community: Ecological Models
  Between Anarchy and Spirituality"), Herford 1980

Dieter **Korzak,** *Neue Formen des Zusammenlebens, Erfolge und
  Schwierigkeiten des Experiments Wohngemeinschaft<*
  ("New Forms of Living Together, Success and Difficulties of
  the Experiment of 'Shared Housing'"), Frankfurt/M.: Fischer
  Verlag 1979

Johann August **Schülein** (Hg.), *Kommunen und Wohngemein-schaften – Der Familie entkommen? Eine Textsammlung* ("Communes and Shared Housing – Escape from the Family? A Collection of Texts"), Gießen: Focus Verlag) 1978, 2nd edition 1979

On architecture

Literature that I purchased in connection with my work on Telotopia:

Jürgen **Tietz**, *Geschichte der Architektur des 20. Jahrhunderts* ("The History of 20th Century Architecture"), Cologne: Könemann 1998

Pete **Nelson**, *New Treehouses of the World*, New York: Harry N. Abrams Publishing 2009

James **Wines**, *Grüne Architektur* ("Green Architecture"), edited by Philip Jodidio, Cologne: Taschen Verlag 2000

Clifford A. **Pearson**, *Modern American Houses: Four Decades of Award-Winning Design in Architectural Record* (New York: Harry N. Abrams 1996)

Published by **Taschen Verlag**, Cologne

Taschen produces books with color images at relatively low prices.

Deidi von **Schaewen** & John **Matzels**, *Fantasy Worlds*, Cologne. Taschen Verlag 1999   - (Extraordinary Constructions)

Charlotte & Peter **Fiell**, *William Morris*, Cologne: 1999
William Morris was a pioneer of "alternative culture" (see Internet). He also wrote a utopian novel entitled *News from Nowhere*

Barbara & René **Stoeltie**, *Landhäuser auf Mallorca* ("Country Houses in Majorca"), Cologne: 2000.

About **Hundertwasser:**
Harry **Rand**, *Hundertwasser*, Cologne 1991
Pierre Restany, *Hundertwasser* (French edition), 1998

Psychologists who have dealt with psychology regarding New Culture, e.g.:

Carl R. **Rogers,** *A Way of Being*, Boston 1980

Erich **Fromm,** *To Have or To Be*, London: Jonathan Cape Ltd 1978 (reprint)

Erich **Fromm,** *Leben zwischen Haben und Sein* ("Living Between Having and Being", by Rainer Funk, ed.), Freiburg - Basel – Vienna 1993

Erich **Fromm,** *Vom Haben zum Sein. Wege und Irrwege der Selbsterfahrung* ("From Having to Being: Ways and Aberrations of Self-Awareness", by Rainer Funk, ed.), Weinheim - Basel 1989, 1991[4]

Horst Eberhard **Richter**, *Lernziel Solidarität* ("Learning Goal: Solidarity") (1974), Reinbek: Rowohlt 1979, 1982

Horst Eberhard **Richter**, *Flüchten oder Standhalten* ("Fleeing or Standing Firm"), Reinbek: Rowohlt 1976

Horst Eberhard **Richter**, *Zur Psychologie des Friedens* ("On the Psychology of Peace", 1982), Reinbek: Rowohlt 1984

Alexander **Lowen**, *The Betrayal of the Body*, New York: Macmillan 1967

M. Scott **Peck**, *Living Utopia – Notes from the Life of a Community*, New York: 1984

Marshall B. **Rosenberg**, *Nonviolent Communication: A Language of Life*, Encinitas, CA: Puddle Dancer Press 2003 (2nd Edition Printing) Harry N. Abrams 2009

Referring **relationships:**

Aaron **Kipnis** & Elizabeth **Herron**,*Gender War, Gender Peace: The Quest for Love and Justice Between Men and Women*, New York: William Morrow and Company, Inc. 1994

Michael Lukas **Moeller**, *Die Liebe ist das Kind der Freiheit* ("Love is the Child of Freedom"), Reinbek bei Hamburg: rororo (Rowohlt) 1990, 16th impr. (Rowohlt 1986)
Other important titles by this author on pair communication

Wolfgang **Schmidbauer**, *Die Angst vor Nähe*("The Fear of Intimacy"), Reinbek: Rowohlt 1985

Gordon **Inkeles** & Murray **Todris**, *Sensuele Massage* (Dutch); Original 1972 San Francisco; NL: Utrecht 1974

Margo **Anand**, *Tantra: The Art of Sexual Ecstasy: The Path of Sacred Sexuality for Western Lovers*, New York: Jeremy P. Tarcher/Putnam 1989 (Softcover)

Philosophy, ethnology, history - e.g.:

Lewis **Mumford**, *The Myth of the Machine, Vol. 1: Technics and Human Development; Vol. 2: The Pentagon of Power*, New York: Harcourt Brace Jovanovich 1966/1967

Ivan Illich, *Tools for Conviviality*, New York: Harper and Row 1973   -   an important book of the 1970s

Institut für Auslandsbeziehungen (Institute for Foreign Relations), Stuttgart & Württembergischer Kunstverein (Arts Council of Württemberg), **Exotische Welten** – Europäische Phantasien ("Exotic Worlds – European Imaginations"), Edition Cantz, Stuttgart 1987 including some exhibitions in Stuttgart 1987)
-contains a lot of material on the complex of Utopia - Colonialism

194

Shuichi **Kato**, *Geheimnis Japan* ("Secret Japan"), Cologne: VGS
   Verlagsgesellschaft 1992   - here only as an example for
                  ethnology, cultural history, and cultural impetus

Chögyam **Trungpa**, *Shambala, The Sacred Path of the Warrior*,
   1984

Joachim-Ernst **Berendt**, *Nada Brahma – Die Welt ist Klang* ("The
   World is Sound"), (Frankfurt/M. 1983), rororo Reinbek bei
   Hamburg: Rowohlt 1983, 1997

Literature cited

Emmanuel **Anati**, *Höhlenmalerei* ("Cave Art"), (1997), Düsseldorf
   2002

Joachim **Bauer**, *Prinzip Menschlichkeit.* Warum wir von Natur aus
   kooperieren ("The Humane Principle: Why We Cooperate
   Naturally") (2006), Pbk: Munich: Heyne 2014 [7]

Martin **Buber**, *Der utopische Sozialismus* ("Utopian Socialism"),
   Cologne 1967

Henning **Christoph**, Klaus E. **Müller** & Ute **Ritz-Müller**, *Soul of
   Africa - Magie eines Kontinents* ("Magic of a Continent"),
   Cologne: 1999

Fiona **Danks** & Jo **Schofield**, *Nature's Playground – Activities,
   Crafts and Games to Encourage Children to Get Outdoors*,
   London: Frances Lincoln Ltd 2005

Jeff **Doring** (Hg.), *Gwion Gwion. Dulwan Mamaa - Secret and
   Sacred Pathways of the Ngarinyin Aboriginal People of
   Australia*, Cologne: Konemann 2000

Erik H. **Erikson**, *Identity and the Life Cycle*, New York:
   International Universities Press, Inc. 1959, 1980 (reprint)

Edoardo **Fazzioli**, *Gemalte Wörter, 214 chinesische Schriftzeichen –* vom Bild zum Begriff, Wiesbaden 2003 (nach der 5. Auflage von 1991; Original Milano 1986)

Erich **Fromm**, *The Art of Loving*, London: Allen & Unwin 1979

Eluan **Ghazal**, *Der heilige Tanz, Orientalischer Tanz und sakrale Erotik*, (Berlin 1995) München 1999 Originaltitel????

Daniel **Goleman**, Paul **Kaufman** & Michael **Ray**, *The Creative Spirit* (1996), New York: Penguin Books 1993

Jane **Goodall** (& Philipp Berman), *Reason for Hope - Autobiography*, London: Time Warner 1999

Michael **Haerdter** & Sumie **Kawaim,** Butoh. *Die Rebellion des Körpers – Ein Tanz aus Japan* ("Butoh: The Body's Rebellion – A Dance from Japan"), Berlin 1986, 3rd edition 1998

Peter Michael **Hamel**, *Durch Musik zum Selbst* ("Accessing Your Self Through Music"), Bern – München – Wien, 1976

Harenberg Lexikon der Religionen, *Die Religionen und Glaubensgemeinschaften der Welt* (Religions and Religious Communities of the World"), ed. by Berthold **Budde** and Christine **Laue-Bothen**, Dortmund 2002

Johan **Huizinga**, *Homo Ludens, Vom Ursprung der Kultur im Spiel* ("The Origin of Culture in Play"), Hamburg, (1956), 1981

Gerald **Hüther**, *Was wir sind und was wir sein könnten – Ein neurobiologischer Mutmacher* ("What We Are and What We Could Be – A Neurobiological Encouragement"), Frankfurt/M.: S. Fischer Verlag 2011; Fischer Taschenbuch 2013, 2017 [8]

Gerald **Hüther** & Christoph **Quarch**, *Rettet das Spiel! Weil Leben mehr als Funktionieren ist* ("Save Playing! Because Life is More Than Functioning"), Munich: Hanser Verlag 2016

Klaus **Lankheit**, *Documentary new edition of: Wassily Kadinsky, Franz Marc, Der Blaue Reiter*, Munich 1965, revised new edition 1984 (1994)

Roger **Lewin**, *Human Evolution - An Illustrated Introduction*, Malden, MA: Blackwell Science 1999 (fourth edition)

Jean **Liedloff,** *The Continuum Concept*, Duckworth 1975; revised edition London: Penguin Books 1986

Ilse **Loesch**, *Mit Leib und Seele. Erlebte Vergangenheit des Ausdruckstanzes* ("Body and Soul: Experienced Past of Expressive Dancing") , East Berlin 1990

Helma **Marx**, *Das Buch der Mythen (aller Zeiten aller Völker)* ("The Book of Myths (of All Ages and All Peoples"), Graz, Vienna: Verlag Styria, Cologne & Eugen Diederichs Verlag Munich, 1999

John **McCrone**, *The Ape That Spoke: Language and the Evolution of the Human Mind*, New York: William Morrow and Company, Inc. 1991

Reinhold **Messner**, *Dolomiten* ["Dolomites"] (Tappeiner Verlag [possibly Merano/ Italy], revised edition 2004

Daniel **Popp** & Jean-Luc **Manaud**, *Die Wüste leuchtet. Zu Fuß durch die Sahara* ("The Desert is Shining: On Foot Through the Sahara), Munich 2001

Horst Eberhard **Richter**, *Flüchten oder Standhalten* ("Fleeing or Standing Firm"), Reinbek bei Hamburg: Rowohlt (1956), 1981: Rowohlt 1976

Oliver **Sacks,** *The Man Who Mistook His Wife for a Hat*, New York HarperPerennial 1985

Wolf **Schneider**, *Wir Neandertaler – Der abenteuerliche Aufstieg des Menschengeschlechts* ("We Neanderthals – The Adventurous Rise of the Human Race"), (Hamburg, Gütersloh n.d.)

Manfred **Spitzer**, *Lernen: Gehirnforschung und die Schule des Lebens* ("Learning: Brain research and the school of life"), Heidelberg – Berlin: Spektrum Akademischer Verlag (2002), corrected edition 2003

Antje **Tesche-Mentzen** & Herlinde **Koelbl**, *Kunst von Kindern* ("Art by Children"), Munich, 2002

Henry David **Thoreau**, Walden, or Life in the Woods, New York: The Viking Press 1947 (reprint)

Désirée v. **Trotha**, *Heisse Sonne Kalter Mond. Tuareg-Nomaden in der Sahara* ("Hot Sun Cold Moon: Tuareg Nomads in the Sahara"), Munich 2001, 2n edition 2002

Frank Robert **Vivelo**, *Cultural Anthropology: A Basic Introduction,* New York: MacGraw-Hill 1978, reissue: Lanham - New York - London: University Press of America 1994

Literature by Christoph W. Rosenthal

- **Die Humanevolution war ganz anders** – Eine überfällige Revision ("Human Evolution was Very Different - An Overdue Revision"), Remscheid 2018 (Version 1.1 March 2019)

- **Zur Evolution von Selbststeuerung, Liebe, Kommunikation & Kultur** ("On the Evolution of Self-Regulation, Love, Communication, and Culture"), January 2021

- **Die kopernikanische Wende unseres Weltgeschichts-Bildes** *("The Copernican Revolution of Our Image of World History"),* Remscheid 2018 (Version 1.1 January 2021)

- **Die Mesolithische Revolution** – Die Begründung der historischen Entwicklung ("The Mesolithic Revolution – Explaining Historical Evolution"), Rediroma, January 2021

- **Kulturologie.** Die Wissenschaft bzgl. der Software-Struktur des Menschen ("Culturology: The Science Regarding the Software Structure of Man"), May 2021

- **Historiologie.** Die Wissenschaft bzgl. der Systematiken der historischen Entwicklung und ihrer Effekte für die menschliche Existenz („Historiology. The science regarding systematics of historical development and their effects upon human existence"). 2023

- **Cûl Tura: Die Entzifferung und Rekonstruktion der ursprünglichen Sprache des Menschen (**"Cûl Tura: The Decoding and reconstruction of Man's Original Language")

Band 1: Die ursprüngliche Sprache des Homo sapiens ("The Original Language of Homo Sapiens"). 2021

Band 2: Der Ursprung unserer Wörter. Teilbände a/b ("The Origin of Our Words. Parts a/b") 2021

Band 3: Ursprachlich und frühgeschichtlich orientiertes Herkunfts-wörterbuch des Deutschen („Etymological Dictionary Regarding the Primeval Language and Early Historical Language of German") 2024

Band 4: Was eigentliche Sprache ist. Zur Evolution von Sprache und zur historischen >babylonischen Sprachverwirrung< („What Actual Language Is. On the Evolution of Language and on the Historical "Babylonian Linguistic Confusion"). 2023

Band 5: Vom Wunder und Abenteuer des Lebens (Of the Wonder and Adventure of Life"). 2024

Band 6: >Frau Holle und der Drache von Lascaux<. Zur Entzifferung der eiszeitlichen Symbolik und Sprache des Homo sapiens ("Mother Holle and the Dragon of Lascaux". On the Decoding of Ice Age Symbolism and the Language of Homo sapiens"). 2021

Band 7: Mebuntu: Die erste historische Sprachform (Mebentu: The First Historical Form of Language). 2021

Band 8: Unser Wortschatz der Frühzeit (Our Vocabulary of the Early Period). 2024

Edition Neue Kultur

(Edition New Culture)

Materials on history and the New Culture
A label of the New Culture workshop

www.edition-neue-kultur.de

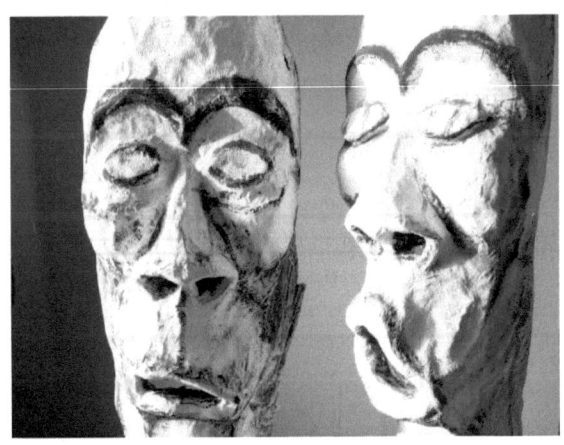